## Praise for BULLIES, TYRANTS, AND IMPOSSIBLE PEOPLE

"None of us—whether in sports, the corporate world, entertainment, government or private life—is immune to the destructive effects of clashing personalities. With remarkable ease in this must-read book, Ron Shapiro and Mark Jankowski have cracked the case of one of our most frustrating yet inescapable daily challenges."

—BILL BELICHICK

"Throughout my career, I have always considered myself a born salesman, but inconsistent when dealing with bullies. I have known Ron for years and have had the privilege of personally witnessing him disarm impossible people. Finally, Ron has presented his tried and true methods in this book for anyone wanting that edge over life's difficult people. Any skepticism you may have will disappear if you implement and practice these accomplished techniques."

—STEPHEN BISCIOTTI, cofounder, Allegis Group, and owner, Baltimore Ravens

"Ron and Mark have been educating MBNA for years using their straightforward approach. *Bullies, Tyrants, and Impossible People* is easy to comprehend, relevant in many ways, and effective at improving performance. Whether you are educating a sales force, managers, or front-line company representatives, or just looking to improve your own skills at dealing with difficult people, this book is a great resource."

—JOHN R. COCHRAN, CEO, MBNA America Bank, NA

"In a world increasingly full of bluster, hype, and exaggerated conflict, Ron Shapiro has always been a calm voice of reason, advancing the interests of those he represents without resorting to the tone or tactics of those he faces. Here, he and his partner, Mark Jankowski, share their techniques for creating workable solutions when dealing with even the most difficult of people."

—BOB COSTAS

"In this easy-to-read work full of stories, strategies, and solutions, Shapiro and Jankowski teach us how to disarm and outmaneuver the various types of difficult people while holding the high ground of decency. Using the N.I.C.E. principles that have made them America's premier seminar teachers, they show us how to master the troublemakers without becoming one. No wonder corporate America is impressed. Do yourself a favor and buy this book!"

—JOANN DAVIS, author of *The Little Secret That Can Change Your Life*

"Mastering the principles and doing the exercises in Ron Shapiro and Mark Jankowski's new book will help you develop the skills needed to navigate through minefields of difficult people and unfair circumstances, anxiety-provoking affairs in which the outcome really matters. My prescription for my friends who must voyage through these challenging straits is to read this book! It could be the best investment you make this year."

—J. RAYMOND DePAULO, JR., M.D., chairman, Department of Psychiatry and Behavioral Sciences, Johns Hopkins University School of Medicine

"This book is an invaluable tool to help anyone in business or otherwise deal with difficult personalities and situations. Make no mistake about it, the reader will be better prepared to deal with life's day-to-day confrontations more effectively."

—CARLOS EVANS, wholesale banking executive, Wachovia Bank

"*Bullies, Tyrants, and Impossible People* provides great insight and guidance on how to deal with difficult people effectively. The tools and examples Ron and Mark share offer thoughtful means of moving potentially disastrous encounters to productive conclusions and ultimately successful relationships. Readers of this book will develop a new level of understanding about human behavior. A must-read!"

—SUSAN C. KEATING, president and CEO, National Foundation for Credit Counseling

"Once again, Ron Shapiro and Mark Jankowski demonstrate their uncanny feel for how relationships work. They provide clear and practical guidance as to how to deal with and master tough scenarios. Ron Shapiro is an all-world negotiator and person. I treasure this book because it allows me to continue to learn from him. You will too."

—RANDY LEVINE, president, New York Yankees

"When dealing with bullies, tyrants, and impossible people, I've always employed my own very effective strategy: I ask Ron Shapiro to do it for me. Ron has been my lawyer, advisor, agent, and good friend for twenty-one years. Now, with this very enlightening and entertaining book replete with stories about Dirty Harry, Gandhi, George Steinbrenner, and many others, Ron and Mark teach us all how it's done."

—JON MILLER, voice of ESPN's *Sunday Night Baseball*

"This book is complete with exciting real-life stories from guys who specialize in the business of dealing with difficulty. Ironically, the day I finished the book, I found myself in conflict with an apparent bully, and before reverting to habit, I recalled and implemented Ron's masterful techniques to defuse the situation. Colleagues who witnessed the circumstances asked in awe, 'How'd you do that?' I told them the same thing I advise you: Read this book!"

—STEVE MOSKO, president, Sony Pictures Television

"In our personal and professional lives, we all encounter difficult people, situations, and environments. Knowing how to work with others without compromising one's standard in values is a difficult balance. The N.I.C.E. system that Ron Shapiro and Mark Jankowski describe in this book is a practical four-point system that can be applied to all aspects of life."

—WILLIE RANDOLPH, manager, New York Mets

"Ron has always had a gift for dealing with people and gaining great results under the most difficult circumstances. This book is very insightful and helps build skills for those times when we have to work with the most difficult of people. It is a valuable tool for anyone wishing to improve on this inevitable aspect of life."

—CAL RIPKEN JR.

"Big-city mayors encounter their fair share of 'impossible people,' and one of the greatest things about this book is that I actually watched the authors apply their ideas in solving difficult urban problems. Understanding how to deal effectively with people can define success or failure for any elected official. This book is the guide to achieving that understanding."

—KURT L. SCHMOKE, former mayor of Baltimore and dean of
Howard University School of Law

# Bullies, Tyrants, and Impossible People

*How to Beat Them Without Joining Them*

## RONALD M. SHAPIRO &
## MARK A. JANKOWSKI

*with James Dale*

THREE RIVERS PRESS • NEW YORK

Published in the United States by Three Rivers Press, an imprint of the
Crown Publishing Group, a division of Random House, Inc., New York.
www.crownpublishing.com

Three Rivers Press and the Tugoat design are registered trademarks of
Random House, Inc.

Originally published in hardcover in the United States by Crown Business,
an imprint of the Crown Publishing Group, a division of Random House, Inc.,
New York, in 2005.

Library of Congress Cataloging-in-Publication Data
Shapiro, Ronald M.
Bullies, tyrants, and impossible people: how to beat them without joining them /
Ronald M. Shapiro and Mark A. Jankowski, with James Dale.—1st ed.
1. Interpersonal conflict. I. Jankowski, Mark A. II. Dale, James. III. Title.
BF637.I48S53 2005
303.6'9—dc22          2004029027

ISBN 978-1-4000-5012-3

*Design by Robert C. Olsson*

First Paperback Edition

146028962

*To my love, Cathi,
and to our wonderful children and grandchildren—
may they live in a world with fewer tyrants and bullies.*

—RMS

*To my dad for showing me the path. To my mom for getting me
started. To my siblings for leading the way. To my friends for
making it fun. To Lori, Jack, Anna, and Rosa
for putting it all in perspective.*

—MAJ

# CONTENTS

## PART ONE

## The N.I.C.E. System for Battling Bullies, Tyrants, and Impossible People

## PART TWO

## N—Neutralize Your Emotions: Learning to Act Rather Than React

PART THREE

## I—Identify Types:
## Know What Kind of "Difficult" You're Up Against

PART FOUR

## C—Control the Encounter: Shaping the Outcome

PART FIVE

## E—Explore Options: Getting "Unstuck"

# ONCE UPON A DEAL . . .
## *(A grim fairy tale with a happy ending)*

ONCE UPON A TIME, there was an infamous corporate raider— let's call him B.B.W.—who preyed on companies with good products but weak management. He was known as a bully who simply blew away anyone or anything in his way. The mere threat of his involvement was often enough to make management fold without a fight. B.B.W. would take over, fire staff, slash product quality, and suck profits out until the company's reputation was destroyed, and then he'd move on to his next target.

One of his early victims was a company that used a straw-and-hay composite to build low-cost (but not very durable) housing. B.B.W. employed his usual threats and coercion and sure enough, the president, F.L.P., waved the white flag before the battle had even begun. B.B.W. decimated overhead, gutted quality control, and reaped windfall (though temporary) profits.

Full of his own success and more intimidating than ever, B.B.W. set his sights on a developer of rustic wooden homes. B.B.W. bullied until the company management, led by entrepreneur S.L.P., panicked and surrendered. True to form, B.B.W. swept in, cut operations to the bone, and squeezed out short-term gains.

Feeling unstoppable, B.B.W. took aim at a bigger target, a company that constructed sturdy brick ranch homes. Company founder, T.L.P., was a savvy businessman who had studied B.B.W.'s past techniques. T.L.P. didn't take B.B.W.'s vicious methods personally. Instead, he asked questions, assessed B.B.W.'s strengths and his own, considered various scenarios, and planned responses for each. After fair consideration, T.L.P. politely declined B.B.W.'s overtures. B.B.W. doubled his hostile efforts, pressuring other investors, threatening legal action, and lobbying board members. Finally, B.B.W. pressed for a board vote on his takeover offer. T.L.P. made his case—that the company would be stripped bare, bled dry for profits, and discarded, as was B.B.W.'s modus operandi. The board voted to remain independent.

B.B.W.'s conglomerate, now drained of critical assets, floundered until he was forced to sell. The buyer? T.L.P.'s company, which restored the component companies to financial health.

B.B.W.'s deal-making style was, in a word, bullying. It had always seemed to work. That is, until he encountered an adversary who understood how and why B.B.W.'s techniques worked and knew how to deal with them.

---

If the story sounds familiar, it should. It's *The Three Little Pigs*. As you may recall, the Big Bad Wolf (B.B.W.) huffed and puffed and blew in the straw house of the First Little Pig (F.L.P.), did likewise with the wood house of the Second Little Pig (S.L.P.), but ran into a brick wall, so to speak, when it came to the house of the Third Little Pig (T.L.P.) and ended up a casualty by trying a hostile entry via the chimney. The Third Little Pig understood how to deal with life's Big Bad Wolves. And that's just what we intend to teach you—how to get what you want from difficult people without becoming one of them.

In this book, we'll show you how to harness the power of what we call N.I.C.E., to outnegotiate, outsmart, outmaneuver, outlast, outlogic, outthink, and outwin life's bullies, tyrants, and impossible people—without becoming one of them yourself. We'll show you how to do it while not losing your cool (unless you mean to do so as a tactic to get what you're after). We'll show you how to do it while maintaining your integrity. We'll show you how to do it without surrendering, sacrificing, giving up, or giving in. And we'll show you how to do it in business life, social life, and family life.

First, we will teach you how to get what you want—in a deal, negotiation, transaction, contract, sale, encounter, or conversation— no matter how difficult the person on the other side of the table, desk, phone, computer, or backyard fence, and we will teach you how to do this without waving the white flag, running away, or becoming impossible yourself.

Second, we will teach you a systematic approach to getting what you want based on the acronym N.I.C.E.:

**N**eutralize your emotions
**I**dentify type
**C**ontrol the encounter
**E**xplore options

Third, we will arm you with tools and exercises to help you assess your own strengths and weaknesses in dealing with difficult people.

Finally, we will teach by anecdote, that is, by bringing lessons to life with actual cases. We'll offer real-world stories—on buying and selling, staff management, cultivating talent, lobbying positions, marketing products and services, motivating employees, winning raises, winning friends, wooing dates, and getting along with in-laws—from business deals (within both Fortune 500 companies and family-owned businesses), labor-management impasses, sports contracts, and strikes to who-blinks-first showdowns with stars, agents, producers, and studio bosses. These stories of deals struck and deals lost will illustrate and demonstrate how the N.I.C.E. system works and how you can apply it in your own difficult situations.

## PART ONE

# The N.I.C.E. System for Battling Bullies, Tyrants, and Impossible People

---

# CHAPTER ONE

# N.I.C.E.

*How to Beat Them Without Joining Them*

## BULLIES, TYRANTS, AND IMPOSSIBLE PEOPLE ARE EVERYWHERE

THEY'RE AT THE OFFICE, down the street, at the mall, on an airplane, in the checkout line, in the next highway lane, on the Internet, on the phone. They're male, female, old and crotchety, young and feisty, strangers, relatives, and even people who call themselves friends. Sometimes it seems like everywhere you turn, there's another one: your nothing-you-do-is-good-enough boss, your no-price-is-ever-low-enough client, the next-door neighbor whose dog barks all night, the guy at the movies who sits between two empty seats and won't move over so you and your friend can sit together, the maître d' who looks through you like you don't exist, the granite-hearted lost-baggage attendant, the meter maid who sees you running up with change but won't stop writing that ticket, the piggish developer who'd rather lose the property than share the profit, the purchasing agent who pits suppliers against one another until one crumples, the broker whose commission is more important than the sale, the chief executive officer (C.E.O.) whose fragile ego is all that matters.

Life's difficult people can make everyday life hell. Every conversation is a conflict. Every sale is a test. Every contract is a headache.

Every meeting is a battle. Every deal is a war. They make life difficult, if not impossible. They even tempt you to become one of
them. Fight fire with fire, stubborn with stubborn, anger with anger,
temper with temper, ego with ego. But that rarely works. It usually
just brings an unpleasant situation to an unsatisfying end.

## YOU'RE NICE. SO WHAT?

You're a nice person. Maybe not every hour of every day, but in
general you're basically nice or try to be or, at least, want others to
think you're nice. And there are plenty of others like you: people
who have their ups and downs, people who don't want to be seen
as pushovers, people who are deal breakers, who have short tempers, points they won't bend on, "matters of principle," or even
occasional bouts of plain old stubbornness. In the end, however,
most of us "nice people" find a way to work out our differences
in the confrontations of life, whether they're business encounters,
social situations, or family issues.

If the person with whom you interact is reasonable, rational, and sensible, resolutions are relatively simple. Sure, some issues may be challenging, some take longer than others to resolve,
some are complicated, even temporarily aggravating, but usually
you find a way. You each give and take, listen and learn, and find
enough common ground to reach a conclusion.

But—and this is a big but—what happens when you face
someone who *isn't* nice, who *doesn't* try to be nice, or who *doesn't*
*care* whether other people think he or she is nice or not? What do
you do when you come across a really impossible person (and
there are plenty of them)? Then what, Mr. Nice Guy? When the
other side isn't sensible or reasonable or sane, how do you resolve

your issues, make a deal, settle a dispute, or decide where to have dinner? When you find yourself across the table, backyard, room, or phone line from a truly nasty, difficult, even irrational individual, then what are your choices?

A. Give up? Run for cover, close your eyes, and wait until it's over? If she attacks from the get-go, do you wave the white flag and surrender? If she blindsides you the moment you let your guard down, do you turn the other cheek and get clobbered on the other cheek?

B. Get nasty back? Must you stop being nice and turn nasty, difficult, and irrational yourself? Must you turn even nastier, more difficult, and less rational than she is?

C. Find another alternative? Is there a "nice" way to get what you want?

## N.I.C.E.—THE ANTIDOTE TO B.T.I.P. (BULLIES, TYRANTS, AND IMPOSSIBLE PEOPLE)

The next person you encounter may be difficult, angry, irrational, emotional, demanding, close-minded, tyrannical, illogical, rude, or all of the above and as a result can create a personal encounter that is dreaded, feared, hated, upsetting, intimidating, challenging, distasteful, disgusting, offensive, stomach-churning, or all of the above. Many of us would rather make no deal, have no meeting, not sit down, and even avoid all contact than face one of these types. But we can't just put our heads in the sand and hope the problems and problem people go away.

That's why we created N.I.C.E.

N—Neutralize emotions
I—Identify type
C—Control the encounter
E—Explore options

N.I.C.E. is a systematic approach for successfully dealing with all of life's most difficult people *without becoming one of them.* It's simple, proven, and applicable to virtually any type of difficult person and any difficult situation.

---

# N.I.C.E.

## THE SYSTEM AND HOW IT WORKS

**N**—Neutralize your emotions. Dealing with difficult people can be an emotional challenge. The more emotional you are, the less rational you behave. Conversely, the more your emotions are in check, the more you can be in control of a positive outcome.

**I**—Identify the type. There are three basic types of difficult people (and several permutations of each).

- The Situationally Difficult: those people whose situation or circumstances make them difficult
- The Strategically Difficult: those people who believe being unreasonable is effective
- The Simply Difficult: those people with an ingrained personality characteristic

---

C—Control the encounter. Once you know which type of difficult individual you face, you can employ the appropriate techniques to help shape and determine the outcome of the encounter. If you utilize the right techniques, you can change the fate of deals, meetings, and everyday confrontations.

E—Explore options. Even after shaping the encounter, you may still be at an impasse. The process of getting "unstuck" often requires the development of options—alternative solutions—so both sides can give and get. (This includes the option of ending without escalating, reserved for those instances in which the best deal is no deal, which can preserve the possibility of a future deal.)

Our system is a sensible, logical, sound approach but, until you fully understand and practice it, not always easy to apply. Emotions don't necessarily respond to logic. Types are hard to pinpoint and may be multiple types at once. Creative options are elusive and require real creativity. And escalated ends can be tempting. The process requires analysis and steadfast discipline. Never forget you are facing a challenge, a human obstacle, a walking talking barrier to civil exchange or progress, someone who, knowingly or unconsciously, does not make things easy.

B.T.I.P. are those whose behavior is reactive, manipulative, uncooperative, or some combination of these characteristics. Examples: high-profile types like Idi Amin and Saddam Hussein, mythical types like the Big Bad Wolf, or everyday types like an impolite waiter.

People often *think* that a nice person is someone whose behavior is malleable, passive, or excessively accommodating. Examples: Mr. Rogers, the ambassador of a weak country at the United Nations, or the teacher's pet.

But the way we define a N.I.C.E. person is someone who is focused, assertive, and resourceful. Examples: Nelson Mandela, Gandhi, Henry Kissinger, Warren Buffet, Joe Montana—diplomats, steady successes, cool and composed athletes.

Let's make it very clear that being N.I.C.E. does *not* mean being a wimp or pushover. By using the systematic approach, a N.I.C.E. person is someone who is going to get his or her way *without* becoming a B.T.I.P.

Don't give in to the temptation to just react. Use the systematic approach—N.I.C.E.

## N.I.C.E.—NOT JUST A THEORY BUT A SYSTEMATIC APPROACH WITH PROVEN RESULTS

N.I.C.E. is a systematic approach, that is, a set of practical tactics tested, modified, refined, and ultimately proven, over and over, in real-life business and social encounters, events, negotiations, deals, showdowns, standoffs, and human confrontations. Don't go out in the world without it.

The N.I.C.E. system works for the following reasons:

- It enables you to know, almost automatically, what to do *before* you encounter a difficult person or situation.
- It helps you practice putting new, more effective, nondefensive habits in place.
- It helps you understand what you did right or wrong in a situation so that you can learn from your successes and failures and not repeat your mistakes.

# CHAPTER TWO

# The Civil Rights Lawyer
# Who Lost His Cool and His Case

*If You Don't Rule Your Emotions, They Will Rule You*

THE FIRST LETTER and first tenet of N.I.C.E. indicates the critical importance of maintaining your composure when dealing with a difficult person. Difficult people tend to act in ways that cause us to react. By definition, reacting means we have lost control. We aren't methodically taking wise or intelligent or analytical action. Instead, reflex has taken over. Reflexes may be natural, but they aren't always desirable. We get hit in the kneecap and our leg kicks. We get hit with an insult and we insult back. We get hit with an unreasonable demand and we refuse to budge. Progress stops.

The better you are at neutralizing your emotions and maintaining (or regaining) composure during a confrontation, the more you're in control and can employ effective tactics. Emotions are not tactics. They are involuntary demonstrations of feelings. Try to save those for happy weddings and sad movies.

Difficult people are like the dishes on the menu with the little red pepper symbol next to them. It's a warning that you may get burned. Take an antacid. Neutralize, neutralize, neutralize.

What follows is a story of Ron's that dramatically demonstrates what *not* to do when your emotions are being tested. He didn't maintain his composure; he stewed. He didn't regain control; he boiled. He didn't neutralize; he burned.

## THE CIVIL RIGHTS LAWYER WHO LOST HIS COOL AND HIS CASE
### *Failure to Neutralize Emotions*

For graduating law students entering the workforce, the late 1960s/ early 1970s were a preview to the dotcom 1990s. In other words, it was a sellers' market. We young lawyers were the valuable commodities, and the law firms were the buyers. I was fortunate enough to be "selling" myself with a cum laude law degree from Harvard; I received offers from several firms and ultimately accepted a position with a prominent firm. The offer not only included a good salary for the times (a fraction of what the 1990s would bring) but, equally important, the opportunity to "do whatever you wanted to do," that is, whatever area of the law most stimulated a young attorney. For me, that meant civil rights cases. As long as I agreed to work on a minimum number of securities cases, I could fill the rest of my time with pro bono (no income to the firm) civil rights litigation.

Working on behalf of an organization called Baltimore Neighborhoods, Inc., my area of focus became the desegregation of previously segregated apartment units in the city of Baltimore. Though these were not situations of de jure (or "by law") discrimination, since those laws had been overturned, they were often apparent cases of de facto (or "in fact") discrimination. There were a number of apartment complexes that used questionable excuses or forms of manipulation to deny renting to African Americans.

To determine that a particular housing complex was discriminating, we would send in "testers," or potential renters whose profiles were identical except for race. We had some success through this tactic in desegregating several apartments and were making good progress.

Then, using a pair of testers we called the "two Carols," we took on an apartment complex called the Balmoral. The testers were volunteers, people who believed deeply in what we were fighting for and who donated their time by acting as prototype renters at various housing developments. Not only did these testers have like incomes, like jobs, and like single status, but they were also, coincidentally, both named Carol, one white, one black. The white Carol was told by the building manager that there were several apartment units available and was given her choice of those units. However, the black Carol was told no more units were available and was rejected. We brought suit under a number of different civil rights acts, including one passed just after the Civil War, which had been upheld by the highest courts as creating a private right of action for housing discrimination claims such as ours.

Our case was brought before Judge R. Dorsey Watkins in the United States District Court for the District of Maryland. Judge Watkins was known by those in the courthouse as a man who held traditional, perhaps old-fashioned, ideals. The word around the courthouse was that Judge Watkins was something of a strict constructionist and not given to expansive readings of statutes and decisions. Nevertheless, I was youthfully hopeful the judge would see justice in my case.

The moment the case began, however, I sensed my hopes were in trouble. In my opening argument, I stated that we were bringing the case under the 1866 Civil Rights Act and was summarily halted by Judge Watkins, who demanded to know how I saw the case as a basis of authority for desegregating housing (something judges often and rightfully do). Was he doubting my case? My precedent? My ace-in-the-hole? I was shocked. Was I hearing him right? Impossible. Not only I, but other civil rights lawyers as well were certain that the Supreme Court had made the precedent eminently clear. What was Judge Watkins trying to tell me?

I stifled my temper and tried to explain. "Your Honor, the case of *Jones v. Mayer,* decided by the Supreme Court, has made clear that this is the result mandated under the law." While I can't remember his exact words, I can remember my feelings when he dismissed my argument and me with something to the effect of "Mr. Shapiro, it's not a matter of what you think that Court has said, it's a matter of what this court is saying. And this court is questioning whether that case makes the 1866 Civil Rights Act applicable to a circumstance such as this. We will pass on that issue for now and get on with your case."

Though I now understand Judge Watkins was questioning certain aspects of my interpretation of *Jones v. Mayer* (rather than the Supreme Court's application) with respect to housing desegregation, because I was so emotionally charged at the time, I perceived him to be *attacking* my case, and the Supreme Court's holding in *Jones v. Mayer,* which supported my case!

The judge's attack ate at me. I feared any hopes I'd held for fairness were on the endangered list. I felt my emotions escalating from irritation to annoyance to seething rage as I interpreted Judge Watkins's views as standing between me and what I perceived as a just result. I suppose I began to think that if he didn't accept my view of the opinion of nine wise, respected, gray-haired men of the Supreme Court, what chance did a young, liberal, idealistic civil rights lawyer have? Not much, as it turned out.

During the presentation of my case, the judge began to impugn the testimony of my testers, the two Carols. He grilled, he doubted, and he challenged; I was amazed. Why? What had these two done other than try to rent an apartment? What ulterior motive did they have? All they did was recount the events. Why was he going after them? As the case came to a close, the answer to all of those questions became clear. Judge Watkins concluded that the two Carols were, in his words, "not truth-tellers." His rationale was that if they would allow themselves to be used as testers by Baltimore Neighborhoods, Inc.—that is, "play the part of renters" rather than actually being renters—they might cross the line between truth and falsehood. Judge Watkins simply doubted the credibility of the Carols. If I had been getting hot before, my emotional temperature now climbed into the high-fever range; I was hot and my emotions were nearly combustible. I objected. He overruled. I objected again. He overruled again. I countered that the natural extension of his logic would undermine all efforts of the I.R.S., F.B.I., and all other law enforcement agencies that use undercover agents (or non-truth-tellers) to expose major criminal activity. He would hear none of it. As Judge Watkins and I knew, I was not there debating I.R.S. and F.B.I. procedures but rather the Balmoral's discriminatory practices. I could only think, Mind closed, case closed.

Because of my relative inexperience in the courtroom, one of the firm's partners and outstanding trial lawyers, Lawrence Rodowsky (who later became a judge of the Court of Appeals of Maryland, Maryland's highest court), supported me on the case. Larry's backing was especially meaningful because he was more conservative than I was in social-political outlook. Even as the judge made his harsh arguments against my position and made it clear he was not going to rule in our favor, Larry was sympathetic and supportive and encouraged me to accept the outcome calmly. He was a man who rarely, if ever, lost control. The same cannot be said of his youthful, strong-willed, idealistic, unbending, liberal-minded side-kick: me.

When the unfavorable ruling came down, whatever outward efforts I'd made to hide my mood dissolved. I scowled, I frowned, I glared, I glowered. I turned and gave my clients a hug in defeat and stormed out of the courtroom. Then I launched into an all-night research foray in an attempt to find any means possible to tear down the judge's ruling and build a case for appeal. I read the law books. I searched for rulings. I made calls to experts. I poured over materials. I reviewed and relived our entire case. I'd love to say that just like in the movies, in the wee hours my driven, relentless investigation uncovered the little-known case that turned the situation from disaster to victory. No such happy ending. I stayed up all night, fueled by emotion, collapsed on the law library table until morning, and, I think, woke up with the impression of a big law book on my cheek. This was a classic case of *not* neutralizing emotions when facing a difficult adversary.

Had I neutralized my emotions sooner, while in court, I would have had the occasion and capacity to ask Judge Watkins to help me understand his concerns about my case and his interpretation of a *Jones v. Mayer* precedent as well as his evaluation of my testers. Instead, because I didn't neutralize my emotions, I fumed, lost perspective, and immediately made Judge Watkins out to be my adversary rather than the fact finder and judgment maker.

### What Might Ron Do Differently Today? Almost Everything.

- He would have employed N.I.C.E.
- He would have been ready for the tactics that tempt one to take attacks personally.

- He would have utilized the techniques that counter those tactics (more about those later).
- He certainly would have recognized where the outcome of the case was headed earlier.
- He would have asked for a recess and put his head together with the cooler head of Larry Rodowsky.
- Most important, he would have come up with an entirely different strategy.

### The Lesson: Neutralize your emotions for more effective actions.

After you've neutralized your emotions, what's next? You have to learn to identify the type of difficult person you're facing.

# CHAPTER THREE

# First Lock All Your Vendors in a Small Room

*Know Who You're Dealing with
or You'll Never Know How to Deal with Them*

DIFFICULT PEOPLE—B.T.I.P.—come in infinite varieties and permutations of personality, profession, looks, traits, and styles: charming but dishonest, greedy but smart, sweet on the outside but hard on the inside, intimidating, coy, temperamental but kind, temperamental but mean, dumb like a fox, just plain dumb, egomaniacal, craving approval, loud and obnoxious, quiet and obnoxious, and on and on. Fortunately, for the purposes of dealing effectively with any and all of them, there are just three basic types of difficult—the Situationally Difficult, the Strategically Difficult, and the Simply Difficult—and we haven't met a person yet who doesn't fall into one of the three categories. Understanding them is the first step to identifying and ultimately overcoming them.

- *The Situationally Difficult.* These people are difficult because *something happened.* These people are not necessarily inherently hard to deal with and in fact may normally be pleasant or at least reasonable, but particular circumstances—from a bad encounter with the boss to a car wreck to visiting in-laws—can turn the benign individual into a temporary terror.

• *The Strategically Difficult.* These people are difficult because *they think that being difficult works.* They believe they have empirical evidence that being difficult as a strategy is the most effective way to get results. The more demanding you are, the more your demands will get met.

• *The Simply Difficult.* These people are difficult because *they are difficult.* It is the central overriding characteristic of their persona. In fact, this behavior is so deeply embedded, these people will even do themselves harm as long as they can do others greater harm. There are very few people who are irretrievably simply difficult, but they definitely exist.

## DIAGNOSIS—THE FIRST STEP TO TREATMENT

Learn to distinguish among the Situationally Difficult, the Strategically Difficult, and the Simply Difficult. Diagnosis is 90 percent of the cure. You have to know what—or who—you're suffering from before you can treat the problem effectively. Know the difference between common cases of the Situationally Difficult, more serious cases of the Strategically Difficult, and the sometimes terminal cases of the Simply Difficult.

The lessons of N.I.C.E. apply to all types of difficult people. Difficult is a matter of degrees. Prepare for the worst. If you're effective with the most difficult, you're even more effective with the semidifficult and not so difficult.

In most instances, the symptoms are pretty clear. As they teach medical students during their training, "When you hear hoofbeats, don't look for zebras."

Here's a true story that illustrates the critical importance of recognizing not just that you are up against a difficult person but exactly what type of difficult that person happens to be. If you don't know what flavor or variety you're facing, you cannot possibly know what to expect, how to react, or how to counteract what you face. And, as you'll see, it's very entertaining to hear what was done—how, when, and where it was done—as long as you weren't the one to whom it was being done.

## FIRST LOCK ALL OF YOUR VENDORS IN A SMALL ROOM; THEN TURN UP THE HEAT
### *Failure to Identify the Type of Difficult Person*

Allegis Group Inc. is a company that since its inception in 1993 practically created the field of supplying temporary consultants and contracting technical personnel. Allegis provides over sixty-five thousand individuals annually to the most sophisticated companies, including most of the Fortune 500, around the world. Needless to say, the field they virtually invented is now a hotly contested category where every contract is a competitive battle.

It was on that combative field that Jim Novick, an Allegis sales executive, experienced his own classic difficult confrontation. It seems that Allegis was pursuing new business by bidding on a contract for a large technical services company, run by a world-renowned business mogul. Jim didn't have any real history of doing business with this titan company. He had no prejudice one way or the other about the methods of its management. He didn't know if he'd be dealing with people who were easygoing, realistic, compromising, hard-nosed, demanding, obstinate, or impossible (much less what variety of difficult). He just knew this was one of the world's leading companies and he wanted to deliver a signed deal to his bosses.

After initial contact had been established between Allegis and the technical services company, a last-minute invitation was proffered to Jim's company. Jim was to fly down the next morning (at his own expense) for an immediate meeting. To paraphrase, the invitation went something like this: "Please send your representative to our corporate headquarters to discuss details of how the two companies might work together." It seemed like it would be a pretty standard meeting to Jim as he packed up his pitch and caught his flight. He'd make his presentation, field some questions, and then the powers that decide such things would undoubtedly compare the Allegis proposal with one or two others and come to a decision. Or so Jim thought.

What he didn't know was that his competitors had also been invited to the corporate headquarters on the very same date to meet in the same room at the exact same time. The whole school of fish would be shot in one barrel. Choose your analogy; the results are equally stacked against the victims.

And Jim didn't know the "negotiating techniques" that would be applied by this behemoth corporation. But the moment Jim walked into that cramped, too small, too hot conference room, he began to get the idea. There were twelve competitive vendors (a.k.a. victims) like him, each in a hard, stiff chair, pulled up to a small table, inches from each other. As if staring in the face of your competitor wasn't enough, sitting behind each vendor was a corporate representative, literally looking over the visitors' shoulders. Then one of the mogul's henchmen went to the thermostat (Thank goodness, Jim thought) and turned it up!

Next, each vendor was asked to make his or her presentation. The vendors had to spell out all the specifics—delivery dates, contingency plans, every detail of how they worked—baring all secrets in front of their archcompetitors. Jim wasn't asked for a business recommendation; instead, the company's representatives told Jim how they were going to do business with him, and if he and Allegis didn't agree, they were excused. Prices were then written on a piece of paper, sealed in an envelope, and handed in. And the whole time there was a corporate detective leaning over them!

Jim says at that moment he felt that he knew what it was like to be the guy on the cop show who gets picked out of a lineup. The "accused perp" is put in a hot box, and the bad cop (or corporate rep) stands behind him as he writes out his confession (or price), all the while grilling, "Are you sure it went down like that? You didn't hurt anybody? You sure you didn't have a gun? Things could go easier if you remembered it a little differently." Jim and the other vendors were in the hot box, each with his or her own private bad cop.

Finally, the humiliation seemed to be over. Wrong. The vendors were then taken to separate rooms where they met with another corporate rep (the good cop). This rep confidentially told each vendor he or she was unlikely to make it to the next round because that vendor's price was higher than the others. But . . . if they could just "lower the price a little bit," they might make it to the final three. Naturally, Jim did everything he could to make his bid better. After a few more concessions were generously suggested by the good cop, and made by Jim, Allegis made the final three.

Now the decision would be made, he thought. Not quite. The "winners" were brought back into the original room, now a few degrees hotter, and asked to make additional presentations and answer more questions, again in front of one another. Jim was told that the executive vice president would come in to detail the process of winning this company's business. Jim was sweating profusely. The V.P. entered, asked each of the three remaining presenters to make additional concessions, and waited for the sweaty group to respond. Jim told the V.P. that he had to talk to his boss, whereby the V.P. scowled at Jim, shot him a bold stare of surprise, rose from his chair, and left the room without shaking his hand. Once more, the vendors were separated out into their hot-box rooms for one more round of "lower your price; you're almost there." It was about this time that Jim thought, Is this contract worth getting? Am I winning or losing if I get this contract?

For better or worse, Allegis did not get the contract. Never mind the contract, Jim thought. He was still reliving the dreadful presentation procedures this notorious corporation employed. It wasn't profitable. It wasn't pleasant. It did not lead to a relationship on which to build future business. But the real lesson was in the style of the encounter. Jim and the other vendors simply didn't know what type of individuals or company they were facing. They kept assuming it would get better. They kept assuming it was almost over. They kept assuming it was just a normal negotiation.

After a final immersion in the corporate oven, Jim finally lost his cool and said, "You know what? We're not going to be treated like this. It's inhumane and we're done here!"

To this day, Jim doesn't know if it was the room temperature or his frustration that put him over the edge, but he was definitely hot under the collar. Jim contends his experience with that company was the most hostile experience he'd ever been in. But he regrets he lost his cool, because if he had maintained his composure instead, he might have someday, somewhere found himself in another situation with the company, in better circumstances or better armed to deal with the circumstances.

### If He Knew Then What He Knows Now . . .

Had Jim possessed the skills to identify the corporation's type of difficult, had he mastered N.I.C.E. before his heated meeting, he could have been the one vendor in the room with the savvy to counter their tactics with his own methods of control. What he and his associates *didn't* know about the types they were facing made all the difference.

- They didn't know if they were dealing with the Situationally Difficult, who had been through a bad bidding experience and had been scarred by it.

or

- They didn't know if they were up against the Strategically Difficult, who had determined that this was a smart, effective methodology for getting the most favorable deals.

or

- They didn't know if they were encountering the Simply Difficult, who were just bad characters, out to do harm and to destroy those with whom they do business.

Had Jim and his counterparts known what type they were facing, they'd have known how to counter the particular techniques instead of being victims to it. (As you will see in upcoming chapters, these were perfect examples of Strategically Difficult people.)

After you identify the type you face, what do you do about it? You have to find a way or ways to counteract or overcome their behavior. That leads to the next element of the N.I.C.E. system— Controlling the Encounter.

# CHAPTER FOUR

# "We Don't Make Change"
## What You Don't Control Often Runs Amok

O NCE YOU'VE DETERMINED what type of difficult person you're up against, you can determine the most effective responses to apply. Armed with the right tools and techniques, you can use them to control or shape the results of the meeting/endeavor/ deal/date/whatever. Controlling the encounter is our proactive process that enables you to regain and/or maintain determination over the final outcome. It is an M.O. for B.T.I.P.

For the Situationally Difficult person, you'll learn the techniques for discovering and then de-escalating the situational escalators. For the Strategically Difficult person, you'll learn how to work within the boundaries of the other person's strategy, actually utilizing his or her rules to find an answer or employing a well-considered counterstrategy. For the Simply Difficult person, you'll learn when and if there is a possibility of solution, where the real power lies, and when the best solution is to walk away.

If you don't control the encounter, it (or the other side) controls you. The circumstances, often set by the other side, are stacked against you. No good outcome is likely to occur. In fact, things will not only be bad, but could get worse. Whether the two parties are countries, families, companies, or spouses, if one party does not respond with the appropriate techniques to control the encounter, positions are only likely to harden and become immovable. Instead of reaching a mutually acceptable outcome, the parties may allow even the smallest of encounters to escalate into warfare. Here's an indelible example from the convenience store scene in the movie *Falling Down.*

## "WE DON'T MAKE CHANGE"
### *Failure to Create Solutions and Options*

If you saw the movie, you may remember that Michael Douglas's character, William Foster, having lost his job, is showing ever-increasing signs of losing his civility. Life's insults are wearing him down.

Now, at the end of his already short fuse, things are about to get even worse. He stops outside a convenience store to make a phone call, a simple undertaking, or so one might think. He steps into the convenience store and asks the Korean proprietor, Mr. Lee, to change a dollar for the pay phone. Mr. Lee replies with his inflexible store policy, "No change. Have to buy or leave."

Foster's fuse burns perilously close to its end. He picks up a cold soda can and rubs it across his perspiring forehead. Lee says, "Eighty-fife cent." Eighty-five cents from a dollar won't leave Foster enough change for a phone call. Foster offers to buy the soda and then, once the cash drawer is open, exchange his fifty cents for the coins he needs. Again, Lee refuses to budge, "Eighty-fife cent. You pay or go." Foster is ready to explode. He attacks Lee's Asian pronunciation, "What's a 'fife'? I don't understand 'fife.' There is a 'v' in the word. It's 'fi-ve.' You don't got 'v's in China?" Lee retorts, "Not Chinese. I'm Korean."

What began as a simple request for change has somehow become a battle of ethnic slurs. Foster goes on a rant. "You come to my country, take my money, and don't even have the grace to learn how to speak my language." Lee, every bit as implacable as Foster, holds his ground. "You go now. No trouble." But Foster has had it. "I stay. What do you think of that?"

Suddenly, there's all-out war. Lee reaches for a stick under the counter. Foster wrestles him to the ground, takes the stick, and smashes a display case. Lee cowers on the floor, whimpering, "Take the money. Take the money." Foster, now self-righteous, rages like a mad dictator. "You think I'm a thief? . . . I'm not the thief. I'm not the one charging eighty-five cents for a stinking soda. You're the thief. I'm just standing up for my rights as a consumer. I'm rolling back prices to 1965." He points the stick at various items in the store and asks the price. "Donuts, package of six. How much?" When Lee responds, "Dollar twelve," Foster knocks the donuts to the floor, shouting, "Too much!" Next he demands the price of aspirin. Lee answers, "Three-forty." Foster smashes the aspirin display. Then he asks how much for four double-A batteries. Lee starts to give the price but, catching on, lowers it in midsentence, "Fi . . . four twenty-nine." Still too high for Foster. He smashes the shelf. Then he holds up the original soda can and asks pointedly, "One soda, twelve ounce?" Lee knows what to say, "Fifty cents." Foster responds, "Sold," opens the cash register, puts a dollar in, and takes out fifty cents in change.

He turns to the door and offers his parting message. "It's been a pleasure frequenting your establishment."

## The Differences Controlling the Encounter Might Have Made

- What if Lee had begun by empathizing rather than opposing Foster, simply asking the obviously agitated

Foster, "What's wrong?" This might have controlled the encounter and changed its outcome altogether. Lee would've recognized that Foster was Situationally Difficult, not abdicated any ground, and allowed Foster to vent and possibly cool down.

• What if Lee had asked Foster the purpose or importance of the call? Again, this might have engaged Foster and possibly lowered his agitation level.

• What if Lee had suggested an item that cost fifty cents or less, such as a mint or gum? This method of controlling the encounter would've responded to Foster's clearly Situationally Difficult behavior, but in a manner that stuck to Lee's no-change policy.

• What if Lee had let Foster use the store phone? Again, Lee could've controlled the encounter and stuck to his deal points—"no change without a purchase"—but prevented Foster's ballistic behavior.

• Given the context of the movie's story, it's hard to imagine the volatile Foster controlling the encounter, but what if he had asked Lee *why* he was rigid in refusing to give change? Had he never been in a similar circumstance? Had he never needed a stranger's assistance? Foster might have tried to engage Lee in conversation, searching for common ground rather than all-out confrontation. Failing that, what if Foster (in a moment of rationality) had asked another customer for change?

There are undoubtedly countless other methods or techniques of controlling the encounter that might have resulted in a less volatile, more satisfactory outcome. But instead, war broke out.

*The Lesson: Control the encounter or it controls you.*

Unfortunately, there are those rare encounters that are *not* going to be resolved with a satisfactory outcome, at least not at the moment. Nonetheless, it is just as important to apply the right tactics to those, because outcomes have a way of changing over time. Which leads to the final element in the N.I.C.E. system— Exploring Options.

# CHAPTER FIVE

# We'll Get You Fired

## *Ultimatums Without Options Lead to Impasses*

Once you've identified the type of difficult individual you're facing and have done your best to control the encounter with the appropriate responses, you may still face an impasse. That's when exploring options can serve to get you "unstuck."

In most dealings it quickly becomes clear what the key issues are and where the sticking points lie. You know what you want and they know what they want, but neither side wants to give up a point or risk losing face by giving in. It isn't just the issues; it's the ego. You're stuck—*unless* you can brainstorm options, ideas, and solutions that dramatically alter or reinvent the rules and, consequently, expectations: change the definition of profit/loss, or change the timetable, or change the definition of success (e.g., so that it is tied to quality, not just price), or change the dynamics of negotiation (e.g., bring in a third party), or change the short-term and long-term goals, or change the length of the deal, or change the renewal or escape clauses, or . . . In other words, create a "menu" of options that can solve the problem and/or let the other person save face in the process.

Unfortunately, however, not all dealing ends with a deal. That's where the ultimate option comes in: ending without escalating.

Know when and how to walk away from a difficult person or encounter. Not all union-management contract talks result in union-management contracts. Not all mergers merge. Not all buyouts get bought. Not all cease-fires cease the firing. Not all neighbors settle who's responsible for the tree on the property line. Not all trial separations are trial. Despite all efforts, sometimes no common ground is found and some resolutions just don't happen. *At least, for now.* But just because an agreement wasn't struck doesn't mean management has to lock out the union or that countries must resume bombing each other or that neighbors have to move away or that husbands and wives can't have amicable divorces. Sometimes the best deal is knowing there is no deal, and walking away without burning bridges leaves open the possibility that there could be a deal, agreement, pact, or other positive outcome at some future time.

It's very tempting, when things get tough, to force a confrontation. We get pushed and pushed and pushed and finally say, "Enough, you can't push me one inch further." Instead of pursuing options or creative alternatives, we pursue showdowns. And then, when all else fails, instead of just ending, we end with escalation, burning bridges (and occasionally blowing them up and scorching the earth beneath). We can learn from those misguided showdowns. Well, at least we can learn the lessons of how *not* to do it, as Ron painfully relives in his true story of a (former) client.

## YOU CAN'T TELL US WHAT TO DO. WE'LL GET YOU FIRED.
### *Failure to Explore Options and Failure to End Without Escalating*

Early in its existence, the Shapiro Negotiations Institute was enjoying an impeccable track record (we knew) and excellent personal relationships (we thought) with a ten-billion-dollar Fortune 500, multinational outsourcing services company. (I've changed all the names, except ours, to protect the innocent. Unfortunately, it's too late to protect us.) This huge corporation—call it Global Mega-Corp—was an acknowledged leader in providing food service, maintenance, uniforms, and management to some of the largest, most visible institutions around the world. My partner, Mark, and I conducted several in-depth, customized negotiations seminars designed to identify business problems or weaknesses, teach techniques for overcoming sales resistance, competition, pricing, and contract "churn," or turnover. Bottom-line proof of our impact was that we were told that, as a result of our seminars, sales went up—measurably so. Contract cancellations went down—measurably so. Old business stayed and new business increased. We were even instrumental in helping the company gain access to business opportunities with key venues throughout Maryland. The chairman of the company had become a personal friend as well as a fan of our first book, *The Power of Nice.* Our results were outstanding and our connections were rock-solid at the very top. We couldn't have been more secure. Famous last words . . .

Because of our success in other divisions, Sam Z., a business unit manager in the Uniform Rental Division, requested that we bid on providing training to his division. He assigned Elvira F., his human resources manager, to oversee the relationship. We were surprised when Elvira said that before she could hire us, we would have to "prove ourselves." (As it turned out, despite her job in human resources, she was hardly human or humane.) We felt that our track record within the company spoke for itself. Nonetheless, we assumed that by doing a short meeting and demonstrating the essence of our program to Elvira, she would then award us the contract. We assumed wrong.

Following our short demo, Elvira initially assured us we would get the business but insisted we first complete one "task," the writing of two customer role-plays, an exercise that we knew would take us over twenty hours to develop. While we normally would not do this much work before being awarded a contract, relying on her assurances that we would ultimately win the contract (and because of our prior track record), we patiently proceeded.

After spending even more than our projected twenty hours working with Mel M., a sales manager from the company, writing and rewriting, we presented the customized role-plays. We were confident that we would now start scheduling our programs.

Instead, we were told to wait. So we waited . . . and waited . . . and waited. Finally, we called Mel and asked him to do some research to see if he could determine what was holding up the process. A day later he called back and told us that Elvira Z. was hiring another training company. As if that was not bad enough, our contact told us that the contract with this competitor had been signed *before* Elvira had even requested us to write the customized role-plays. The coup de grâce, however, was the fact that good old Elvira had given our role-plays to our competitor to use in their course!

We were outraged. How could she do this to us? Didn't she realize who we were? Didn't she know the chairman of the company was a personal fan? Hadn't she seen the bottom-line results? Was she aware we had even turned down competitive business out of loyalty to his company? We were not going to take this sitting down. We'd show her. Since this woman had the nerve to already assign work to another firm, she had essentially fired us. We would respond likewise. We would have her fired.

Mark and I took our case to the highest authority, the chairman. We told him the entire story and said that we did not think that someone so duplicitous should continue to represent his organization (that was our nicer way of saying that she should be fired). Faced with an impasse, we had forced a showdown. It would be Elvira, the not-so-human human resources manager, or us. Right versus wrong. Good versus evil. No creative alternatives. No compromises. No shades of gray. The chairman listened. His brow furrowed and his eyes flashed. He scowled. He even harrumphed. He was properly outraged at this employee's temerity and precipitous behavior. He said he would think it over and get back to us with his conclusions. We left feeling we had taken a difficult but necessary step. We had, after all, been pushed too far.

Not long afterward, the chairman called me. He had thought long and hard on the situation. Elvira Z. was wrong. She had flown in the face of success. She had definitely made a bad decision. It was inexcusable. I responded enthusiastically in violent agreement. The chairman said that he personally spoke to Sam Z., the business unit manager who had originally requested we bid on the new assignment and Elvira's boss. Sam was outraged and said he would "have a serious conversation with this employee." But that would be the extent of the reprimand. (Sam, on behalf of his business unit, later even went so far as to send our organization flowers with an apology.)

The chairman acknowledged that he did not think Sam's rebuke of Elvira was a strong enough punishment, but he went on to say the only thing worse than what this human resources manager did would be for the chairman to override a business unit manager. Bosses don't usurp the power they've invested in key people. The decision, though wrong, would stand.

Mark and I had *almost* gotten Elvira, the human resources manager, fired. But not quite. Instead, we burned a bridge that would prove hard, if not impossible, to rebuild. Second-guessing ourselves, maybe there had been other options: splitting the work with the other vendor, getting additional compensation for the work we had done, providing another type of seminar to that division, and so on. But we had not taken that path. We had opted for showdown. And suffered the consequences.

*Postscript:* Approximately eighteen months later, Elvira decided to "pursue other opportunities" and left the company. That might have presented a renewed opportunity for us if we had not torched our bridges and lost that opportunity.

## Could'ves and Should'ves

In retrospect, we have our *could'ves* and *should'ves*—actions and ideas that maintained our integrity and values but still explored creative solutions for the near or long term.

- We should've neutralized our emotions, realizing that the loss of a contract was not necessarily the loss of a client.
- We should've recognized what kind of person we were dealing with and then responded appropriately— controlling the encounter instead of letting it control us.
- We should've explored the development of ideas, alternatives, and options that might have satisfied both parties—instead of settling for an "us or her" choice.
- We could've sought out counsel from other key players and allies within the company as to how best to handle the situation—to further help us develop options.
- We could even have gone to the chairman to ask his advice on how we should handle the problem, thereby maintaining our integrity without resorting to ultimatums.

• And if these options didn't work, we could've even just swallowed the (temporary) loss and retained a (long-term) positive relationship with the company.

But we didn't. Lesson learned.

*The Lesson: Ultimatums without options*
*often lead to impasses.*

## PART TWO

# N—Neutralize Your Emotions

*Learning to Act Rather Than React*

# CHAPTER SIX

# The Securities Commissioner
*Fight, Flight, or Focus*

## NEUTRALIZE YOUR EMOTIONS, AND LEARN TO ACT, NOT REACT

As MOST OF US well know, if we are in control of our emotions when confronting a difficult individual or individuals, we will conduct ourselves better and achieve better results. Composure equals success. It makes sense. Who could argue with serenity and analysis over impulse and volatility?

But composure is often hard to attain and maintain. After all, you are trying to combat natural reactions in the face of strain, intimidation, anxiety, and even outright rage brought on by an unpleasant, nasty, inflammatory adversary. Nastiness creates stress. Stress can lead us to behavior beyond our control. It happens so fast, we're almost unaware of it. It happens every day, in all aspects of life. In fact, it happens so often, we react over and over, almost in knee-jerk fashion, which is rarely the way we'd wish to react.

Composure may be the foundation of success, but stress is too often the basis for failure.

> *He who angers you, conquers you.*
>
> Sister Elizabeth Kenny,
> when facing skepticism over her
> successful polio treatment

Think of the stress you can face almost daily and how it affects you. Some incidents you can withstand with a modicum of self-discipline. Some get under your skin. And some can drive you to emotional and even erratic behavior. Consider these scenarios. How do you react?

*An annoying telemarketer calls during dinner to sell you a subscription to a magazine you already receive.*

*The guy behind you at the movies talks loudly just as the key to the mystery is revealed.*

*Your coworker steals credit from you for winning a new client. Then she gets a raise to reward her success.*

*Your neighbor cuts a prize rosebush down—your prize rosebush.*

*Your daughter loses the cordless phone. Again.*

*You're about to wrap up a land purchase you've been working on for months. At the closing, the seller jacks up the price.*

*You're supposed to meet your husband for dinner. He shows up two hours late.*

*Someone opens credit cards in your name, runs up huge charges, and you find yourself in an enormous battle with the credit card company.*

*A reckless driver nearly runs you off the highway in a fit of road rage.*

Most of us can deal with the telemarketers and the loud talkers. We may lose patience with the late spouse and the bureaucracy of untangling the identity theft. But even the most easy-tempered and unflappable among us are bound to go haywire over the worker who steals credit and the life-threatening driver. As a result, our own behavior will not be as controlled, wise, or effective as it should be. We're only human.

So the question isn't how *not* to have human reactions; it's how to *manage* those reactions so you're the one in control instead of being controlled by the stressor.

## FIGHT OR FLIGHT?

Think about what happens when you are suddenly confronted by a grizzly bear. Oh, you've never had the pleasure? Okay, immediately go out to the woods, find a grizzly bear and antagonize him into coming right at you . . . or just use your imagination. What do you *imagine* happens when you're face-to-face with an angry grizzly bear? He growls. He bares his teeth. He backs you into a corner of his little neck of the woods. You break into a cold sweat. Your heart pounds so loud you can hear it. Your adrenaline floods through your body. Do you stand your ground or head for the hills to see if you can outrun a bear?

Okay, chances are you are not going to be confronted by a grizzly bear. But you may well be confronted by a grizzly boss. What happens then? You probably don't have to use your imagination for this one. Just re-create the scene from memory. He fires questions. He pounds the desk. He backs you into a corner of his wood-paneled office. (He might even bare his teeth.) You break into a cold sweat. Your heart pounds so loud you can hear it. Your adrenaline floods through your body. Do you stand your ground or head for the halls and hide in your office?

In both instances, you are faced with the fight-or-flight responses. We all face bears every day. Some are big and hairy. Others are paunchy and wear suits. But they're both intimidating. What do you do? Why? How do you keep from just having a reflex reaction?

## WHY NOT FIGHT?

For most of us, when stress hits we have one of two responses: fight or flight. In other words, we either instantly go into battle mode with the person on the other side of the table/room/phone/ argument, unleashing unfiltered, untempered, uncensored feelings and reactions, or we avoid trouble altogether by running, literally (feet on pavement) or figuratively (head in sand) from unpleasant reality.

The fight response is almost never a good one, because when we're upset our emotions rule us and we are apt to blurt out what we feel at that exact moment.

*Stop bothering me.*
*Shut up.*
*Get out of my face.*
*You don't care about me.*
*No fair!*
*Why are you picking on me?*
*If you don't like it, too bad.*
*Oh yeah?*
*I hate you.*

Heat-of-the-moment responses are rarely measured, smart, thought out, clever, rational arguments or counterarguments, compromises, or persuasive points of view. Fight responses also often escalate stressful situations. Someone got you upset. You said something back that got the other person upset. Then the other person one-upped your inflammatory comment by raising the emotional stakes even higher. And you called and raised again. And so on. Until neither of you wants anything to do with the other.

The fight response is so visceral, so reflexive, that even the most educated, polished, polite professional people fall prey to it. It's hard to fight the fight instinct. But it rarely gets the results one is after.

## WHY NOT TAKE FLIGHT?

The flight response is not much better than the fight reflex. Running away does nothing about the actual problem. It will still be there when and if you ever come back. And putting your head in the sand, ostrich-style, may give you a close-up view of tiny grains of sand but no insight into how to solve the issue at hand. You have either abdicated to the other person or you've brought any and all potential progress to a standstill. You certainly haven't made your points or explained your position. On the contrary, your message not only doesn't get across, but you may just leave an overall negative impression. You've simply established that you or your side may wither and/or withdraw in the face of strong confrontation.

Surprisingly, important, strong, well-connected people, companies, and entities of stature often opt for flight, thinking it is their only alternative to a knock-down, drag-out fight response. Out of options, they flee, hoping to send a dramatic message by vacating the troubled area.

## FIGHT, FLIGHT . . . OR FIND A BETTER WAY

What responses can you have besides fight or flight? Neutralize. That means you consciously change your emotional responses from automatic or reflex outcomes to controlled or managed behavior. Neutralize your emotions and, instead of reactions, you have actions; instead of retorts, rejoinders, and retaliation, you have initiatives, ideas, and influence.

## FOCUS (A BETTER WAY)

How do you neutralize? By focusing. Consciously sharpen your view of the real issue. Define it, isolate it, stick to it, refuse to be sucked into the emotional distractions, block out everything else, rivet yourself to the issue, the issue, and nothing but the issue. You won't get caught up in a battle. You won't surrender your position. You won't hide. You will focus—maintain and retain your composure—and take on the issue itself. And you will get better results. Ron's personal experience prosecuting a fraudulent securities company illustrates the temptations of fight or flight and the better option, to focus.

## THE SECURITIES COMMISSIONER VERSUS THE FRAUDULENT COMMODITIES BROKERS (AND THEIR ARMY OF FANCY LAWYERS)

Before there were the Michael Milkens, the Ivan Boeskys, the Imclones, or the Enrons, there was a precursor to all of them, a company I took on called First Federated Commodities.

At one time in my career, I served as the securities commissioner of the State of Maryland. By way of background, the commissioner's role, in the years preceding, was an innocuous job that with perhaps one exception had never been an activist position. The job description is to regulate investment and business activities within the state, concurrent with the jurisdiction of federal securities laws. Within Maryland, however, the department comprised the commissioner (at the time, me), the assistant commissioner (who handled filings and other clerical functions), and a part-time assistant attorney general, which made the oversight of all investment and business activity a tall order, often a job that could be done only in a cursory manner. When there was an issue of enforcement—for example, if I came upon a case that might be fraudulent or in some way highly improper—the challenge could become overwhelming. It was me (and whatever help I could muster) against the world. I had to be investment cop, investment lawyer, negotiator, coordinator, and often photocopier–filer–appointment maker. I was wearing so many hats I could have been a Dr. Seuss character.

Soon after being appointed, I got a call from an individual who reported that he had invested several thousand dollars in what had been described to him as a "surefire commodity options deal." Never mind that he should have been suspicious of anything called surefire in the world of investments. He had clearly been misled. He had been given a flowery and highly optimistic pitch, with promises of fantastic returns. Needless to say, the bottom line was that nothing he'd been told comported with reality. Furthermore, he suspected that not only he but many other investors as well were being bilked by those who had taken him in.

The company that had "sold him" used very powerful, persuasive advertising as well as high-pressure tactics. It was a classic boiler-room operation, filled with hard-driving, relentless, slick salespeople. As cops often say, this one "smelled bad," about as bad as a deal could.

So I went to work. I made some initial calls and inquiries and discovered early on that this case had all the characteristics of a true scheme, an overt attempt to bilk people out of their assets. After some evidence gathering, I contacted the principals of the company and informed them that I was going to begin enforcement proceedings against them. I explained that I suspected that there were not only civil liabilities involved but potential criminal conduct as well.

As was my personal style even then, in a gesture toward an open airing of the facts, I offered to meet with them rather than just lowering the axe. Because they were con men, they relished the idea of a meeting. This would be their chance to sell me on their legitimacy and all the good they were accomplishing on behalf of their investors. Of course, they would meet me accompanied by their team of lawyers, who happened to be affiliated with one of the more established and sizable firms in Baltimore.

When they came to visit me in my modest, government-issue office of the securities commissioner, their group comprised the two business principals, two or three of their attorneys, and a couple of their assistants. On my side of the table, there was me. We embarked on a series of meetings, which were at first superficially friendly. They even made an early attempt to persuade me of the legitimate value of their commodity options business. I wasn't buying.

Shortly, the meetings deteriorated into chess games wherein they attempted to intimidate me with their size, prestige, and sheer clout. During the course of the meetings, I told them what I had found through my research and investigation and what I felt I could prove in court. I explained that I was going to issue an order against them but before doing so offered them the chance to voluntarily enter into a civil consent decree that would immediately prevent them from selling any additional commodity options. I even offered them the opportunity to avoid admitting or denying any charges but to simply cease activity. However, I did leave open the issue of financial restitution.

They seemed to view me with what I recall as petty annoyance, sort of like a buzzing mosquito—irritating but not really threatening. In the supercilious fashion that bullies often display to flaunt their intimidation of the opposition, they condescendingly informed me they were confident I could prove nothing. They made it very clear that they could, and would, outmuscle me with bodies, research, paperwork, and legal talent. At some point, they even threatened that they might sue me if I moved forward with any action whatsoever against them. They never spelled out what they would sue me for, but I can only assume it was a not very thinly veiled threat of defamation of their clients' character. Their threats, veiled and overt, didn't end there. It came out in later testimony by one of the investors that when he had raised questions to a principal of the company about business practices, the principal asked the investor if he "remembered *The Godfather* movie," a none-too-subtle message to back off or suffer the consequences.

Looking back, I realize I might have played out either of two classic reactions: I could've had the reflex "Oh, yeah?" response. You can't scare me. I'm angry. I'd rather go down in flames than let you bully me (even if it means I'm not mounting the most rational offensive I could). In other words, the fight reaction. Or I could have felt intimidated, as one country often does when faced with what feels like superior firepower on the other side. Intimidation can lead to surrender, even before the first bullet is fired. I see troops marching, tanks rolling, and missiles ready to launch. I wave the white flag. To put it in nonmilitary terms, in everyday confrontations what goes through your mind is a panicked internal conversation: "How can I ever handle this? What am I going to do? They're going to crush me and I just don't have the capabilities to handle it. I better give up now and just get it over with." In other words, the flight reaction.

Instead, what I did was to step back and carefully think through the situation. I cleared my head, divorced myself from emotion, and performed an honest assessment. In other words, I focused. Although I was short on manpower, I was long on law power, both in terms of how the law would be applied in such cases and in terms of my own understanding of recent interpretations of the law. For example, in a previous meeting, the other side had maintained that commodity options were not securities and therefore not even subject to my regulation. It so happened that I had done a lot of writing and research in that area, including authoring an article entitled "What Is a Security?" ultimately published in the *ABA Journal.* After a full and dispassionate analysis of the strengths, weaknesses, cases, precedents, and facts, my assessment was that despite their view of the law, which I determined to be skewed, my office (i.e., me) could take them on and make a strong, compelling case. Focus enabled me to see reality and make a rational decision.

Once I had focused, the manner in which I took them on was to maintain what I would call a neutralized state throughout the procedure. What this means is that I retained focus by neutralizing a lot of my natural emotional reactions. First, I had to neutralize myself to their air of arrogance toward me, which almost taunted me to lash out and fight, a constant test of self-control. Had I given in to that temptation to fight, I could have used the power of my position as securities commissioner to simply issue an order against the company without going through the judicial system: "You are hereby ordered to stop selling fraudulent commodity options." I could have given it to the press and it would have made a big splash. But I felt that kind of a preemptive reaction would have the weakest legal base to it. It might have made me feel good for a moment, but it would not make for the strongest case. Second, I had to neutralize myself against my own fear of "How the hell am I going to manage this process as big as it is, and an opponent as big as they are?" I knew I was taking on what was probably the biggest fraud case to come out of the State of Maryland in a long time. I could have been overwhelmed by the sheer scope of the case. I could have opted to cut a deal with the other side, a slap on the wrist for the company but, in reality, a defeat for the consumer.

What I did was focus on the resources I had, not on the resources they had. From the standpoint of cold, hard logic, I focused on the law and how it applied favorably to the case. I reached out to people in the legal community, friends of mine, and the attorney general's office, which couldn't give me additional people but could offer expertise and advice. But I focused on a less tangible aspect as well, pure will. I had the will to work, the drive and belief to pursue the case to its end. (Intangible assets are never to be minimized. A true believer is always a more challenging opponent than a hired gun.) The intangible power of will came to tangible fruition in the complaints I drafted, orders I got from judges, and, eventually, in the decisions rendered.

I should note that I was not, up to this point in my career, a real litigator. But this turned out to be my shining moment in the courtroom. I remember going before Judge Proctor in a beautiful, ornate old courthouse in Towson, Maryland, where I set out our case. I was one lawyer with one assistant at a table, and on the other side of the room was a battery of lawyers, law clerks, and expensively tailored clients at another table. But it took only this one lawyer to completely throw the other side off their game. I persuaded a judge to issue a temporary restraining order, effectively halting their entire trading operation until a full hearing could be held. The order put them out of business, at least temporarily. My focus kept me in the game, so to speak.

Then, fueled by that early victory, I went on to make our complete case. Every aspect of their scheme was brought to light, from their high-pressure sales tactics, to their gross overpromises of returns, to their *Godfather*-style threats to investors.

Virtually every detail of the case was a lesson in the value of focus over fight or flight. The bottom line was the judge ruled that commodities were in fact within the purview of the securities commissioner, and, furthermore, he ruled on the merits in our favor and against the defendants. Focus overcame the reactions of fight or flight, helped me put away the "bad guys," and literally won the day. The end . . . or almost.

That wasn't even the end for the defendants. Later they faced criminal prosecution, led not by me but by the U.S. postal authorities. The postal inspectors made the case that this was a fraud utilizing the U.S. mail. I'll never forget that day I went to federal court where I was to testify in the proceedings. By then, instead of seeing a phalanx of arrogant lawyers, with their arrogant lackeys, all serving their arrogant clients, I saw two incarcerated individuals come into court in chains, having been transported from the local jailhouse. To say the least, their demeanor had changed radically.

## FOCUS LIKE AN ATHLETE

Another way to look at fight or flight versus focus is to look at great athletes. When you take on an opponent, you're like a running back being pursued by tacklers, or a batter facing an intimidating pitcher. As a runner, you could fall down before the tacklers tackle you. You could run right into them. Or you can focus on the field, see opportunity, and run that route without distraction. When the pitcher "dusts you off" with an inside fastball, you could lean in and get hit and start a brawl. You could back off and get called out on strikes. Or you can focus, stand your ground, and see nothing but that 99 m.p.h. pitch as you bring your bat around to meet it. You are an athlete, of sorts, facing opposition that would like to intimidate you into fighting or fleeing. Great athletes focus.

## DON'T COUNTERSTRIKE—DISARM

When Phil Jackson was coaching the Chicago Bulls, he recounted in *Inc.* magazine how his players learned that the best way to overcome someone who is attacking you, emotionally or otherwise, is to replace the impulse to strike back with the impulse to become more focused on the game. Jackson recounted that when the Bulls played the Detroit Pistons in the late 1980s, Detroit would win because the Pistons were able to incite the Bulls into fighting back. It was not until the Bulls learned to control their "strike-back" impulse that they were able to overcome the Pistons. As Jackson recalled, "Everybody on our team was slammed around . . . Players were tackled, tripped, elbowed, and smacked in the face. But they all laughed it off. The Pistons didn't know how to respond. We completely disarmed them by not striking back. At that moment, our players became true champions."

---

# CHAPTER SEVEN

# He Called Me the Scum of the Earth

*Change Your Physiology and You Change Your Psychology*

## STRESS, THE ENEMY OF NEUTRALIZING EMOTIONS

Each person reacts to stress differently. It is important to understand your own hot buttons. We all have a sort of built-in meter to pick up on stress. It's a matter of tuning in to ourselves to detect the level of stress as it's occurring so that we have time to suppress and redirect it. Once detected, there are tools we can use to neutralize our emotions and begin to act instead of react.

How do you alter your instinctive responses to stress or neutralize your emotions? There are two ways: changing your physiology and changing your psychology.

## CHANGE YOUR PHYSIOLOGY

### Wrongly Attacked, You Retreat

Let's say you feel unjustly attacked by a supervisor (e.g., teacher, parent, commanding officer, department manager) who misinterpreted a report you prepared and criticizes your work. Your feelings are hurt, but in addition you will experience physical manifestations of discomfort that will further fuel your hurt feelings. The supervisor yells. You withdraw and even take a step or two away from him. He reads errors from your report, out loud, in front of peers. You breathe faster. A coworker makes a comment under her breath to another worker. You're embarrassed and your body temperature rises a bit. No wonder you don't feel you can intelligently and calmly counter your supervisor's incorrect assessment of your work. Your physiology is actually upping your stress level.

What can you do? How can you reverse the escalation? How can you stop natural physical reactions?

## Wrongly Attacked, You Regain Control

There actually are steps you can take to directly affect your physiology. For example, if you practice simple breathing exercises, you can start to inhale and exhale rhythmically when under pressure, rather than hyperventilating. Or you can change the pressure of the moment by changing the venue. Move the conversation to a quieter place, out of the hallway and into an office. You can create breaks or pauses in the momentum of an incident by taking a sip of water, asking a question, or offering the other person a seat. Change the place and/or the pace and you may change the eventual outcome of the encounter. The mere fact that you are the one initiating these steps begins to put you back in control. While you sip the water, you have time to process in your mind how the supervisor got the wrong impression from the report, and this may enable you to answer his criticism before it becomes full-blown. Moving to another location may allow you to point out the misunderstanding in private, rather than the middle of the hallway. Egos are tender in public but more open in private.

Techniques, Habits, and Exercises—Specifics on How the Process Works
Have you ever noticed it's really hard to stay angry when you're
smiling? Okay, you're thinking that when you're smiling, you're
not angry. And when you're angry, you're not smiling. It's not always true. Think of it this way. You're in a store and you're getting
really upset with a surly salesperson who won't let you return a
powder blue sweater that's three sizes too big because you don't
have the receipt. You explain that it was a gift from your mom so
you have no receipt. She asks why your own mom would buy a
sweater three sizes too big. You have no idea. You just want to return the sweater. She asks if perhaps you wore the sweater and
stretched it into its huge size. You swear that you never wore the
sweater. You don't even like powder blue sweaters. She asks why
your mom wouldn't know that you don't like powder blue. You're
exasperated. She says, in cases of questionable returns, you have to
go up two floors to the administrative office for an authorization.
You're losing it. Then your friend, who has been watching the
whole transaction, wisecracks that it would be easier to get top-
level security clearance at the C.I.A. You laugh, despite your aggravation. You find his observation humorous and you have the
involuntary response of laughing. The moment you do, your anger
seems to dissipate, also involuntarily. And that doesn't mean you
have to make a joke to change your mood. Just a pleasant thought
or respite can do the trick. Good humor, a short break, a change of
subject, or the entrance of a third party can all counteract anger.

*The Little Smile Technique* Here's an actual case history of an
athlete facing real pressure and a wise but unconventional coach
and his secret weapon. And it's also the story of how Ron got his
wrought-up Little Leaguer son to relax on the pitcher's mound.

## THIS MAY NOT WORK IN THE MAJOR LEAGUES . . .
## BUT IT WORKED IN LITTLE LEAGUE

When my son, David, was a pitcher for his Little League team, he would concentrate so hard on throwing strikes that he'd get very tense, and instead of pitching better, he'd begin to lose control and start to throw wild pitches. The more tense he got, the less he found the strike zone. After a game or two with too many hits and runs for the opposing team (which is saying a lot in always high-scoring Little League), I thought maybe I should try to help. Instead of giving David technical advice like "Change your stance to the catcher or shorten your windup" or "Come down from the top before you release," I told him to remind himself to smile when he was on the mound. Baseball is supposed to be fun. Sometimes you forget that and get caught up in the pressure and have to remind yourself. I told him that I'd help remind him. After that, game after game, I'd stand at the sidelines, and to the amusement of other parents, I'd cheer him on with "Smile it up, David. Smile it up," until I'd finally see a smile creep across his face. And right after the smile came the strikes.

On the other hand, the reverse can happen. While a smile may make your performance turn positive, a negative outlook can cause negative results. If you're happy but then close your eyes and recall a depressing thought, it's likely your body will absorb and reflect that thought. Your smile will fade, your shoulders will slump, your head will bow, and you may even hunch over or draw inward.

*The Finger-on-the-Lip Habit* An incredibly simple but effective device to stave off negative behavior—doing the wrong things and, particularly, saying the wrong thing—is to keep your mouth closed. It's a good idea but often hard to carry out. Mark explains how he developed a physical gesture that helps make it a habit.

## "SHUT UP, MARK," I SAY TO MYSELF

Someone says something provocative to me, and guess what? It works. I get provoked. Someone challenges. I accept. Someone yells. I yell back. But I don't always yell back the most persuasive, brilliant, or effective retort. In other words, I found there were too many times when I spoke before thinking. I shot from the lip. And almost immediately afterward, I wished I had buttoned, zipped, or Velcroed my lip. So I started consciously buttoning it *in advance,* the moment a conversation even starts to get the least bit tense. Whenever my radar senses a challenging situation, my index finger drifts up to my mouth and comes to rest vertically across both lips. To anyone else, it just looks like I'm thinking—which I am. I'm thinking about not saying something stupid or inflammatory. It makes me literally close my mouth and pause. Not only am I thinking, but I am also physically reminding myself to keep my lips closed until I know exactly how I want to respond. At first I had to remind myself to do it, but now it's become such a habit that it's an automatic reflex. Someone challenges. Finger to the lips. I think. Someone yells. Finger to the lips. Then I respond. And I don't regret what I say (as much).

*The Mood-Behavior Connection* Physical behavior is often the body's manifestation or reflection of one's mood or psychology.

And don't think this is an adult phenomenon. It begins almost from birth. Remember when your two-year-old announced that he had successfully "gone potty" (that is, *in* the potty). No doubt, his little chest thrust out and he stood taller than his usual two foot three. (Even dogs wag their tails when fed and slink away when scolded.) Emotional states tend to equate to physical states and vice versa. It is hardly surprising that changes in your emotions can change your physiology and that your physiology can change your emotions. This isn't just anecdotal or perceived; it's scientific. Witness what this former Johns Hopkins Medicine professor observed.

## TALKING RAISES YOUR BLOOD PRESSURE (BUT LISTENING CAN LOWER IT)

Psychologist James J. Lynch, director of the Life Care Health Center and former faculty member at Johns Hopkins University School of Medicine, is one of the first researchers to use a technology that measures patients' blood pressure, almost word by word, during conversation. What he discovered is something we have long sensed, that speaking has an identifiable, measurable effect on our bodies, specifically on our cardiovascular systems. Put simply, talking tends to cause blood pressure to rise and it continues to climb until the speaker senses that he or she has been heard or understood. Sometimes, of course, that never occurs, leaving the speaker not only frustrated but with markedly increased blood pressure.

Lynch first observed this in crying babies. Adults react just like crying babies except that we have learned to socialize without crying (most of the time). As with babies, when adults are heard (or comforted), their blood pressure tends to decrease. Lynch says, "The biggest misconception . . . is that talking is a mental process. You . . . talk with every cell in your body."

The bottom line is that while talking without feeling you are communicating or "getting through" can raise blood pressure (and possibly do physical harm), the converse is also true. When the relationship between talker and audience or listener is positive, it can be healing. Both parties communicate and derive a psychological as well as physical benefit.

Psychological circumstances can result in a variety of physical manifestations.

When you're facing a truly difficult person (intimidating, powerful, unpredictable, threatening, uncooperative, pushy, etc.), your body will give you clues. Your palms may sweat, you could tense your shoulders, or you might lower your head. Frequently, you'll move backward or retreat in a classic flight position. Or, pushed too far, you may even clench your fists. You will literally get your back up. You'll stick out your chin. Then you begin to move forward or attack in a classic fight position. In either case, your body is the barometer of the psychological weather.

---

*When I am upset, I count to ten.*
*When I am very upset, I count to one hundred.*

Thomas Jefferson

## AN EXERCISE: CHANGE YOUR MIND BY CHANGING YOUR BODY

While it isn't automatic or foolproof, it is frequently possible to actually alter your emotions by altering your physical position, posture, or bearing. Take the situation described earlier in which smiling involuntarily allowed anger to dissipate. What if you smiled on purpose in such circumstances? What if you forced a smile? Would an artificial smile work just like a real one? More pointedly, as in medical treatments with placebos, what is artificial and what is real? If you conjured up a humorous thought, a simply relaxing image, or a calming reflection, the conjured notion might just change your mood. In fact, most times it would. You can force yourself to smile/relax/calm your way out of a bad mood. Try it.

*Caution:* You're only human. This exercise runs counter to the feeling you're having at the moment. It requires you to contradict your own reactions. So, obviously, it takes practice and some detachment. But it does work. No, you can't smile your way out of tragedy. But you can smile your way out of aggravation.

The key to beginning to deal with difficult people—whether they are Situationally, Strategically, or Simply Difficult—is neutralizing the negative impact of your own emotions. To do so, you must learn to recognize these physiological changes that are caused by the stress of encountering difficult people and then employ techniques to counteract these changes. The following techniques, when mastered, can enable you to do just that. They can put you back in control of circumstances.

- Slowing your pace
- Lowering your voice
- Changing your physical environment
- Taking a deep breath

- Relaxing your shoulders
- Smiling
- Putting your finger to your lips
- Asking questions
- Listening
- Counting silently

## CHANGE YOUR PSYCHOLOGY

Before you can begin to affect your own psychology while dealing with others, particularly difficult people, you must first understand what prevents your having self-control of your own psychology. Why can't a rational person simply recognize that he or she is under pressure or stress or is reacting less than optimally and adjust his or her own behavior accordingly? Why can't we just "snap out of it"? Any computer can make just such an adjustment. Unfortunately, it isn't human.

We humans have ingrained beliefs that block our actions, beliefs so ingrained that we don't even recognize them. We just do what they say. They're like fences around rational adjustment. We call these limiting beliefs. And the only way to beat them is to develop and reinforce stronger empowering beliefs.

> *Whether you believe you can or you can't,*
> *you are probably right.*
>
> Henry Ford

## Limiting Beliefs

People who fear or avoid encounters with difficult people often subconsciously have what is termed negative self-talk. It's that little voice in our heads that whispers to us that we cannot do something. It's our personal disaster movie playing on our mental screens. It's the little note of paranoia we write to ourselves. Whatever it is, it capitalizes on all of our insecurities at our most insecure moments, and it cautions and warns and taunts us. Consider these scenarios:

> Today is the day you'll dive off the high board. You climb the ladder. You walk to the end of the board. You look down at the water. Just then, the movie plays in your mind starring you, crawling back to the ladder, clinging to the railing all the way down, whimpering to yourself, "You? You?! You won't. You can't. You knew you never could."

> The boss posts a job opening for a supervisory position. Should you apply? You're qualified. You're ready. Then your little voice says, "Who are you kidding? You're a wimp. A loser. An also-ran."

> You've been studying for your professional certification exam. You know your stuff. You've taken the practice tests. You're ready to walk into the exam room . . . until that little voice takes over. "Not today. Maybe tomorrow. Maybe next year. Maybe it will just go away."

> The repair shop is overcharging you. This work is supposed to be under warranty. They claim these repairs are not covered.

You have to speak up for your rights as a consumer. You tap the very large, very gruff manager on his very broad shoulder. He turns around with a scowl and mutters, "What?" Suddenly a movie scene is playing out in your mind with you shouting to yourself, "Retreat. Surrender. Wave the white flag. Beg for mercy."

Someone cuts in front of you in the checkout line. You should politely tell her that you're next. Instead your little voice dictates a quick note to you: "Back off. That's what you're good at."

You're ready to get out from under your mother's overbearing nature and go out into the world on your own. You get a job, rent an apartment, pack your belongings. As you open the front door, you write the note of insecurity to yourself: "Who are you kidding? You can't live without your mother to take care of you. Turn around. Go to your room. Go to bed. Your mother was right."

You'd like to ask her out. She seems to like you. You walk across the room, open your mouth, but before you can ask her your little voice says to you, "You'll be embarrassed—humiliated—again."

*Disclaimer:* Yes, of course, some limiting beliefs can be helpful. The limiting belief that tells you you cannot step off a building with only an umbrella and float softly to the ground prevents you from having delusions of being Mary Poppins or Evel Knievel.

And some limiting beliefs can even be, in the extreme, debilitating. People with real phobias suffer limiting beliefs that prevent them from getting into an elevator, going outdoors, or flying in an airplane, like the woman in this little story who flew seated next to Ron.

## FEAR OF FLYING
### *A Phobia As the Classic Limiting Belief*

While some people are skeptical about limiting and empowering beliefs and how they impact people's reactions to situations, you only need to observe someone with a phobia to understand how beliefs impact behavior. One time when taking a coast-to-coast flight I sat next to a woman who immediately told me, "I hope you do not mind, but I need the aisle seat because I am afraid of flying." Since I fly so much, I was astonished to see how much this woman's belief that the plane might crash impacted her physically and emotionally. She nearly came to tears when the plane started to taxi down the runway. She would duck and cover her head whenever the plane hit turbulence. She had sweaty palms and a pale complexion. She could barely speak. Even though it was actually quite a pleasant flight and a perfect landing, when we touched down she unclenched the armrests for the first time and said, "Wow—that was a close one."

While this is an extreme example of how beliefs impact behavior, there are many others that are not quite so obvious. It is important, therefore, to understand what your limiting beliefs (or "miniphobias") are. Is it a fear of being wrong? Of not being accepted? Of being taken advantage of? While you may not exhibit the physical symptoms of someone who has a full-fledged phobia, no one can deny that these and other beliefs constantly affect how we think and the way we behave.

Most of our limiting beliefs lie well within the two extremes. They are simply, as the word says, limiting. We might tell ourselves, "I am just not good at math. I shouldn't even bother to try to balance my checkbook," but the result is an overdrawn account, bounced-check charges, and bad credit. By heeding the limiting belief, we're doing ourselves harm. We might say to ourselves, "I'm a lousy speller and it makes people think I'm stupid." Our answer might be to put everything we write through computer spell-checker, a practical solution unless, of course, it results in our losing all confidence to write even the shortest email, Post-it note, or birthday card without running it through a computer program. Then we've created a problem worse than bad spelling—noncommunication.

Since limiting beliefs play on insecurity, it isn't surprising that they often appear under the pressure of dealing with difficult people. What more natural time for inner doubt, pessimism, or self-questioning? You can almost hear your own little voice saying:

> *I am not good at conflict.*
> *I hate confrontation.*
> *I am not as determined as I should be.*
> *I don't even know what I really want.*
> *I don't belong here.*
> *I have a bad temper.*
> *I cry.*
> *I give in too easily.*
> *I do not really deserve any better.*
> *I'm not as smart as the other person.*
> *I tend to screw things up.*

*I'm not the right person for this job.*
*I knew I'd do badly and I was right.*

Admit it. You've probably had one or more of those little conversations in your head in the midst of a stressful encounter. Sometimes you almost feel like the other person—the tougher, more difficult person—is eavesdropping on your tête-à-tête of insecurity and gloating his way through the deal. On the other hand, every one of those limiting beliefs can be slain with a stronger, more potent belief—an empowering belief.

## Empowering Beliefs

People who deal effectively with difficult people either instinctually or through concerted efforts have learned to change that voice in their head. They shut the little wimp up. Or they transform him from a ninety-pound weakling into a black belt in self-confidence. Through practice and specific technique, you can learn to ignore the negative you-can't-do-it voice. You can, instead, listen to your own positive oh-yes-you-can voice.

Rather than chanting the losing mantra of limiting phrases like those above, you can choose to overcome them with positive beliefs. You can create an almost automatic reaction in situations of confrontation in which you invoke your empowering beliefs at the moment of conflict. The more you engage in that practice, the more confidence you'll have. The little voice of limiting beliefs will be silent. The not-so-little voice of empowering beliefs will be shouting these words of encouragement:

*I'm ready.*
*I can handle this situation.*
*I am in control of my own reactions.*

*I've been waiting for this.*
*I will listen and then react accordingly.*
*I have good gut instincts.*
*I've faced this situation before.*
*I will be reasonable.*
*I will show respect and expect respect.*
*I am good at what I do.*
*I'm enjoying this.*

## AN EXERCISE: TRADING BELIEFS

Is the glass half-empty or half-full? Half-empty means why try, it's a lost cause. Half-full means go for it, we're almost there. Outlook makes all the difference in achieving goals.

Here's an exercise in which you purposely create limiting beliefs and practice developing offsetting, empowering beliefs. Look at these examples drawn from real situations and then draw on your life—recent meetings, confrontations, purchases, family issues, financial matters, car repairs—and write down the limiting belief you experienced or would experience in that situation. Then step outside of your limitations and imagine a powerful, positive belief that would meet the limiting belief and overcome it. Like most things in life, if you learn to recognize the negative and get in the habit of reacting with the positive, it will go from exercise to reflex.

Situation: *A young, aspiring actor is going to an audition with the world-renowned film director Steven Spielberg.*
Limiting Belief: *Famous, supersuccessful people intimidate me.*
Empowering Belief: *People are people.*

Situation: *A highly touted rookie running back enters an NFL
   playoff game at a crucial moment. On the other side of the
   line, a grizzled veteran linebacker taunts the rookie.*
Limiting Belief: *I can't handle this pressure.*
Empowering Belief: *I've dealt with tougher people than this guy.*

Situation: *An ad exec is sent to lead her agency's effort to win a
   hotly contested, multimillion-dollar, international ad account
   against the toughest ad agency competitors in the world.*
Limiting Belief: *If I lose, I'll be fired.*
Empowering Belief: *My boss has confidence in me. She knows I'll
   do my best.*

Situation: *An Air Force commander is selected to lead his
   squadron in a bombing mission over territory filled with
   enemy troops and sophisticated ground-to-air weaponry.*
Limiting Belief: *This plan will never work.*
Empowering Belief: *I will find a way to make this work.*

Situation: *A union leader enters contract negotiations with an
   energy company that is demanding major wage concessions.
   Now the company's management is threatening to go to the
   press and claim, without concessions, that the company could
   fold, dealing a devastating blow to the local economy. The fact
   is that the company made record profits, played bookkeeping
   games to hide their success, is in no danger of going under, and
   is just trying to deliver bigger bonuses to greedy execs.*
Limiting Belief: *I become unglued when people use unfair tactics.*
Empowering Belief: *I can always walk away if the deal isn't
   worth making.*

Now think about situations you've been in recently or frequently face in which you are hampered by a limiting belief. Then think of an offsetting empowering belief that would enable you to get past the hurdle or limitation.

> Think work: *What challenge have you had at the office that seemed impossible but in fact could have been undertaken?*
> Think personal life: *What socially intimidating circumstance have you confronted (or avoided confronting) that you might have handled better with an empowering belief?*
> Think family: *What unpleasant duty have you avoided that you could have and should have faced if only you'd been armed with beliefs to counter your limiting feelings?*

## FIGHT, FLIGHT, FOCUS, PSYCHOLOGY, PHYSIOLOGY, NEUTRALIZED EMOTIONS, LIMITING AND EMPOWERING BELIEFS . . . ALL IN ONE STORY

Here is an emotionally charged story in which Ron was presented with the choice of fight, flight, or focus. The situation altered both his psychology and physiology and also challenged him to regain control of both. In the end, his ability to neutralize emotions and replace limiting beliefs with empowering beliefs allowed this extremely difficult and tense encounter to be defused and even have a positive outcome. But Ron's ride was nothing if not an emotional roller coaster.

## HE CALLED ME THE SCUM OF THE EARTH,
## AND IT WENT DOWNHILL FROM THERE
### *Or How a Sports Agent Negotiated with a*
### *General Manager Who Hated Sports Agents*

We conduct negotiation seminars in which people sign up to learn to deal with personal, social, and business challenges more successfully. But the fact is that some of the people are just more willing to learn than others. Some come into the course with certain prejudices that are difficult to overcome. Some, frankly, are looking for confrontation. In other words, we can face difficult people even in our own seminars. Case in point: the guy who called me and my profession the scum of the earth.

In December 1997 Mark and I were in Dallas teaching a program to the National Football League's Management Council, a group comprising team presidents, general managers, and other front-office personnel. Our job was to teach this collection of very experienced deal makers how to use the Power of Nice (as we called our program) to make even better deals. It was a challenging task given the sophistication of the audience; these people negotiate for a living. And it was particularly stimulating for me since before then I had often represented the parties on the other side of the table—the players. To many of the day's participants, I was, in effect, the opposition, the dreaded agent.

While it was a challenge, I didn't expect it to be an ugly showdown. The drama began to unfold almost immediately. I gave my opening remarks, set the stage as to expectations and goals for the day, laid out the agenda, and was just about to get into the meat of the program. Then, in what seemed a split second between my pauses, one member of the audience gathered up years of frustration at the world of players and their agents—escalating pay scales, signing bonuses and guarantees, trade and no-trade clauses, injury protection, free tickets, special meals, special housing, special transportation, what seemed to him to be never-ending demands—and he prepared to let it all out on me.

The gentleman, Bill Polian, one of the leading lights of the NFL and then general manager of the Carolina Panthers, stood up. (I use the term *gentleman* on purpose to illustrate, as you will see, that someone who is normally a gentle man can become a difficult negotiator, owing to certain situations. Understanding that will enable you to deal with the Situationally Difficult negotiator.) I hadn't asked for questions or comments. Bill just rose out of his seat. He had something to say and he was going to say it. The room got quiet. We all watched his anger travel, as if up a thermometer, until his face was as red as his hair. Then he unleashed his hell-fire-and-brimstone tirade—a combination of sarcasm, skepticism, and outright damnation of all representatives of all ballplayers for all time. As best I can recall (as much as I might like to forget), it went something like this: "What are we doing here? Learning to deal with the scum of the earth? Learning from another agent? The Power of *Nice*? [a sarcastic reference to our program]. You must think we're crazy or stupid!"

Murmurs went through the crowd. Several sympathetic eyes looked back at me. But no one spoke. That is, no one except Bill. He wasn't quite finished.

He attempted, in his own angry way, to explain what he meant. "With all due respect and *possibly* with present company excluded, there is no way in hell you can deal with an agent and get a win-win outcome. They exist to screw us and get as much money as they can. They'll lie. They'll cheat. They'll do whatever it takes. Talking about win-win with these jerks doesn't make any sense."

As emotional as he was, he touched a lot of nerves in the audience. There were others in the room who had had bad experiences with agents. Our course teetered on imploding. This was one of those moments of fight or flight.

To tell the truth, I felt I had been hit hard and I was reeling. It hurts when you're attacked. No matter how professional you try to be, you're still human. What could I do? What should I do? A part of me wanted to fight back. "Oh yeah? You want me to believe every general manager is the most honorable individual on earth? Are you guys a bunch of saints? I don't see any halos over your heads. You mean, you aren't out to make the club's bottom line as fat as possible? Doesn't that find its way into your paycheck? Or does it go to charity?"

But I didn't attack. Of course, in a situation like this it may also have been tempting to take flight. I could have had a limiting belief such as "I have no idea how to deal with a heckler." I could have tried to ignore him or even agreed with him, both of which would have undermined my credibility. I knew, rather than fight or take flight, I needed to focus. Take a breath. I did. Change your physiology and you begin to change your psychology. If you take the time to breathe, you can take the time to think. If you can think, you can adjust your attitude. You will realize this is a setback but not necessarily a defeat. No one makes you respond on any timetable other than your own. Take another breath. I did. And I reminded myself that his attack wasn't really personal, despite his choice of words. He hated agents; he didn't hate me. I knew, instinctively, that rather than respond, I should ask questions. I asked, "It sounds like you've had a bad experience with an agent recently. Am I right? Can you tell me about it?"

Bill then launched into a harrowing tale of frustration. It seems that only a couple of months earlier, he had gone through a highly publicized and controversial negotiation with linebacker Kevin Greene and his high-profile agent, Leigh Steinberg. Greene and Steinberg were convinced that given Greene's outstanding career, he was deserving of an immediate pay increase, despite having a year remaining on his two-year contract. Greene was due to earn $650,000 with incentives that would take him to $1.6 million. Polian insisted "a contract is a contract" and the time to renegotiate was when the contract was up. Greene and Steinberg demanded a raise now. They opted for a strategy of "holding out"; that is, Greene refused to practice or play unless his pay was renegotiated. The seventy-four-day holdout resulted in $292,626 in fines, his release from the Panthers, and a football season spent as a professional wrestler. While Polian got his way in terms of sticking to the letter of the contract, it was a lose-lose outcome. The team lost a key player, and Greene lost an important season in his career. The Panthers missed the playoffs, shattering high expectations following the previous season's playoff success. Greene lost fans and respect within the NFL community. It was an ugly incident that left Polian concluding that agents—all agents—don't care about promises, deals, integrity, or honor, only about flagrantly bending, breaking, or disregarding the rules in pursuit of money. As if that weren't enough, two days before the management council met in Dallas, the Carolina Panthers had suffered a devastating loss to the New Orleans Saints, which further fueled Bill's frustration. He hadn't slept the night before and was angry with the management council for insensitively scheduling the council meeting so close to games during the final weeks and the potential playoff push of the season. He had had no time to let his frustrations pass, and the management council meeting only exacerbated those frustrations. So, yes, he was agitated!

While Bill retold his story, I put my finger on my lip and listened intently. I stepped away from the podium. If you feel you're the target, move. Change your physical location and you're in control. Use the time to think again. I walked down the aisle toward Bill. As I listened to his story, I realized this fellow's recent, particularly devastating, negative experience with an agent had left a scar that hadn't yet healed. Maybe he felt he'd lost in that deal, was embarrassed, had been taken advantage of, and swore he'd never be that naïve again.

I changed my psychology from formulating an irrational response by engaging my rational mind and focusing on the facts. The facts:

- This general manager obviously had his reasons to dislike agents.
- In his eyes, I was an agent, de facto the enemy.
- He did not have any actual experience with me as an agent.
- I was being condemned as part of a group. You might say I was a victim of profiling. I fit the description and therefore was not to be trusted. I was the recipient of the totality of all of his agent-dealing frustrations.

I couldn't refute the facts. I couldn't change reality. So how could I find common ground if I was the enemy? Maybe I wasn't always an agent or only an agent. What if sometimes I was a person like Bill Polian? What if I was also management? Maybe I could supplement the facts to dramatically change the situation.

I walked the length of the auditorium to Bill's seat. The whole audience watched. Bill stood glaring at me. I approached. He didn't flinch. The scene had all the characteristics of an Old West showdown. But when I came face-to-face with Bill, I didn't fight with him or fire from the lip. I didn't argue or challenge him or unleash any of the comebacks that flashed through my mind and tempted me. Instead, I leaned over to Bill, microphone in hand, and very quietly said, "I know how you feel." I think I perceived a hint of red draining from his face. He certainly was surprised. An agent agreed with him? But he wasn't giving any ground. He just stared at me as if to say, "What else have you got?" I went on. "I know exactly how you feel. Early in my career, I ran a radio station and I had to negotiate radio personality talent contracts with [I paused dramatically] agents. Some of the agents were not trustworthy. Some were two-faced, duplicitous, and simply immoral. Clearly, some didn't approach the bargaining in a win-win fashion. Some were so shortsighted and greedy that they would suck all the money out of the station for their client even if it jeopardized the success of the station and ultimately the income of that same client."

Before he knew it, Bill was nodding with me, not against me. I knew the same kind of agents he knew.

I kept going. "Some were real bullies or tyrants or worse. But not all of them." Bill studied me carefully. Where was I going? "Some were reasonable. Some had legitimate points to make on behalf of their clients. Some were interested in the financial status of the station. Some wanted to know how their clients could help make the station more successful." Bill nodded reluctantly. I went for the closing argument. "Let me ask you a question, Bill. Is it wise or fair to condemn all for the actions of a few?"

Bill wasn't about to give his ground easily. "Those few are a huge problem."

I continued to find common ground. "I don't disagree with you. But have you *ever* dealt with an agent that you believed you could trust?"

There was a long pause, to say the least. Finally, Bill answered, "Not many."

That's when I knew I had him. "Not many" was better than I hoped for. I was aiming for "one."

I went for the close. "But there were some, Bill?" Bill nodded. The crowd laughed. Bill said, "Yeah, some." As a result of neutralizing, we were on our way to one of the most productive seminars in our history.

*Postscript:* Bill Polian went on to the Indianapolis Colts, where he built one of the strongest organizations in the NFL. That means he signs superstars, deals with their agents, and in order to keep on winning, has to deal with them over and over again. He's done it and continues to do it. I like to think that our interchange that day has played a part.

Even caring, genuine people can allow frustrations to control their emotions and become the Situationally Difficult. Bill Polian is just such an example—a true gentleman whose compounded frustrations and situational difficulties were just too much during our seminar. In fact, later, during a telephone conversation concerning this story, Bill told me that even though he perceived me to be an agent that day, as a baseball fan, he had had a positive impression of my approach to player representation—a win-win approach that he, himself, practices in the NFL.

---

## PART THREE

# I—Identify Types

*Know What Kind of "Difficult" You're Up Against*

# CHAPTER EIGHT

# Close Encounters of the Police Kind
## *Dealing with the Situationally Difficult*

### B.T.I.P. ROTTEN? YES. UNIQUE? NO.

THOUGH THE B.T.I.P. of the world would like to think they're each unique, the plain fact is there are only so many ways to be rotten. Of course, there may be endless ugly character traits, mean gestures, memorably despicable quotes, or perverse habits, but there are limited types. They tend to fall into categories. Tennis star John McEnroe, former Baltimore Colts owner Robert Irsay, Olympic skater Tonya Harding, basketball coach Bobby Knight, British prime minister Winston Churchill, and Russian cold war leader Nikita Khrushchev are all variations on Situationally Difficult hotheads who were known to explode over circumstances. Hall of Famer Ty Cobb, fictional serial killer Hannibal "The Cannibal" Lecter, Red-scare monger Senator Joseph McCarthy, and even former president Richard Nixon were all arguably Strategically Difficult characters who carefully plotted the execution of their vengeful plans. Gangster Al Capone, despotic rulers Idi Amin and the infamous Husseins (Saddam and sons Uday and Qusay), genocidal madmen Joseph Stalin and Adolf Hitler, slaughterer Charles Manson, and perhaps boxer Mike Tyson are all Simply Difficult types who operated on irrationality and pure fear.

And because difficult people of all ilks leave telltale personality prints as specific to them as fingerprints, they can be identified according to category. The trick is learning to spot the obvious or subtle patterns that give them away. The more you know about how they differ, what drives each, and why, the better you will be at dealing with each group.

## 1-2-3 IDENTIFY

Make identification an automatic habit. Follow three simple steps before you get too far into any dealings with someone you suspect may be difficult.

> Research: *Learn about the person, his or her background, style, quirks, characteristics, position, goals, self-image, and reputation. The more you know before you square off, the better prepared and less surprised you will be by behavior.*
>
> Observe: *Each time you encounter the person, watch closely and listen intently. Pick up on the clues in gestures, language, humor, demeanor, anecdotes, social graces—any aspect of character that may indicate the type of individual you're facing.*
>
> Probe and Bond: *If you wonder about what someone thinks or means, how he or she feels, or why, then ask. Be polite and sensitive, but don't be shy and just wonder. People will often just tell you what they mean and why. You may or may not like the answers you get; they can be blunt or even offensive but are often revealing and instructive. Then try to find common ground from which to deal so as to minimize adversarial stances. Though you may be on opposite sides of an issue, what*

*do you and the other person share? Differing politics but similarly aged kids. Buyer versus seller but same alma mater. Unlike business philosophies but like hobbies.*

## THE SITUATIONALLY DIFFICULT

Here's an almost foolproof, exception-proof checklist for identifying the Situationally Difficult person.

✓ They're facing, or just faced, a stressful situation. It could be pressure at work, at home, or even a reaction to world events. It could be money, love, kids, health, time pressure, social forces, or an upcoming confrontation. It could be temporary, recurrent, or constant. But, to the person facing the stress, it is enough to throw their equilibrium out of whack and result in angry, demanding, even irrational responses or demands. And remember, the definition of a stressful situation depends on the person under the stress. What rolls off one person's back can send another over the edge.

✓ They display reactions seemingly out of proportion to events. They may snap at a simple question. They may yell a retort to a calmly spoken statement. They can argue over something that isn't even controversial. Some will storm out of the room and may slam doors, kick chairs, even throw objects. They can turn silent and icy. They can shut off all communication for days. They may issue "do what I say or else" ultimatums. And even if they seem to get their way, they may still refuse to be satisfied (because the stressful situation still exists).

✓ They can be calmed down if handled properly (methods to follow). Despite their reactions to temporal circumstances and overreactions in behavior, they may actually return to very normal and acceptable decorum. A day or so later, one might not know this person was ever difficult or simply wouldn't believe the erratic behavior ascribed to the individual.

In general, the Situationally Difficult person is normally, or at least often, a reasonable individual who becomes difficult to deal with as a result of stress, pressure, or negative events. In other words, a good person in bad circumstances. This individual may have faced any number of challenging situations just prior to or even simultaneous with your encounter.

*She was caught in traffic.*
*He was caught in a lie.*
*She had a fight with her husband.*
*She left her husband.*
*He offered his resignation . . . and the boss accepted it.*
*It's raining (and it's golf day).*
*Mother is moving in.*
*The rent was raised.*
*He received bad health news.*
*Sales quotas were upped.*
*Mice were found in the basement.*
*The house burned down.*
*He's getting transferred.*
*She ran over the neighbor's cat.*
*The V.C.R. didn't tape the game last night.*
*The bank bounced a check.*

Remember the discussion of how we react to various life stresses? Now imagine the person on the other side of the table facing the same kind of stresses or worse. Stresses can range from a honking horn to a devastating medical diagnosis. Some stresses are obvious; some are secret. (Think of all the things we don't know about people we face, and all they don't know about us.) And different people have drastically different thresholds of acceptable stress. Some show their stress. Some keep it inside. Some think they're controlling it only to let it out in unexpected instances. Reactions are often not taken out on the person or persons responsible or on themselves (we rarely blame ourselves). In fact, feelings are almost always released on some other person— maybe on you, if you happen to be the next one in sight or have the misfortune of asking for something and adding to the stress.

## RATIONAL OR IRRATIONAL?

The reactions of Situationally Difficult people are not necessarily irrational. After all, something did go wrong. (Is the bank robber on the Ten Most Wanted list paranoid or just sensible when he feels someone is after him?) But the reactions of situationally affected people are almost always out of proportion to the event or circumstances. The purchasing agent—whose sixteen-year-old son, a brand-new driver, just got in his third accident, which removed the trunk and back seat from the family's minivan—walks into a meeting and your job is to close the sale of fifty prefab office cubicles . . . and by the way, your factory is running behind owing to a production glitch and there's been a substantial price increase. Good luck. If you had your bad news but not his, you'd have a challenging meeting. If you had his but not yours, you'd have a tough time. But given both, you may need a flak jacket.

Try this simple algebra problem: Take the purchasing agent's aggravation resulting from his son's latest automotive adventure (including the bump and paint repairs and the mechanical work and the rental car and the inevitable insurance premium hike and the moving violation—yes, he was speeding at the time . . . ) plus your factory production problem, and then multiply by the price increase and the answer is . . . duck! You're not at a business meeting; you're at a wrestling smack-down, and guess who's going to get smacked. Notice how the situational problems compound on each other. There is no natural de-escalation. Instead, bad news seems to multiply exponentially. And it's very hard to stem the momentum.

The tale that follows recounts a vivid experience that Mark and his family lived through, and it illustrates how innocent circumstances can spiral out of control. What started as an idyllic family outing to the ballpark somehow turned into a nightmare in broad daylight. How? Little by little, one situational factor at a time, until there was a virtual avalanche of negative factors. It's a two-part story. The first part describes the deterioration from pleasant excursion to ugly showdown. The sequel (page 89) reveals the outcome of this situational hell.

## CLOSE ENCOUNTERS OF THE POLICE KIND
### Part I: Parking, Pregnancy, and Police

Once a season the Baltimore Orioles have what they call Run the Bases Day, during which they let kids race around the base paths after the day's game is over. My very pregnant wife, Lori, and I thought it would be great fun to see our three-year-old, Jack, toddle around a major-league infield. We were in a wonderful frame of mind as we drove down to Camden Yards with Jack and his one-year-old sister, Anna.

Knowing the limited attention span of kids, we had decided not to even go to the game until the seventh inning. Unfortunately, that meant our usual parking space was long since gone when we got there and we had to hunt for another spot. As Lori drove, I eyed what looked to be a great space halfway down a block, but there happened to be both No Turn and Do Not Enter signs at the corner. Undeterred (frequently my state of mind), I thought we could slip down the short block unnoticed and told my wife (against her wishes) to make the illegal left turn and enter where it said "Do Not."

She turned, pulled into the spot, and I began to unload the kids. No problem . . . until I saw a police officer give us a big hand wave, which translated roughly as "Do *not* park there. Keep driving." I thought, Okay, we'll just get the kids out here and one of us will go find another space. But when the officer saw us seeming to ignore him, he was sure he had spotted a crime in action. He raced up to our car barking, "License and registration! License and registration!"

Lori then started rummaging through the glove box and found old receipts, car manuals, C.D. cases, maps, napkins, food wrappers, a kiddy-meal toy, directions to her aunt's house, $1.80 in change, and a diaper—but no registration. When the officer glared into her window, she tried to explain, "I'm just trying to drop off my kids." He responded unsympathetically, "I don't care. You're going to get a two-hundred-dollar ticket for doing this." My wife, eight and a half months pregnant and at her emotional acme, began to get upset, first a little, then a lot, eventually hyperventilating, weeping, sobbing, and finally shouting, "I think I'm going into labor!"

For some reason, the police officer seemed to think she was flouting his authority. He got even sterner. "I don't care about that! Just give me your license and registration." I felt I could read my wife's mind: "What do you mean, you don't care about that? Labor is serious. I'm going to have a baby outside the ballpark!" She sobbed harder and louder. Either the police officer heard her or got soaked with tears, because his next reaction was to overreact. "Okay, I'm calling an ambulance to take you to the hospital." He then mumbled police-speak into his walkie-talkie, calling for an ambulance. Lori said, "I don't need an ambulance. I need to calm down." He countered, "No, ma'am, sit right there. You're getting an ambulance." She said, " I just need to walk around." He ordered her, "Do not go anywhere. You're getting an ambulance!" She practically screamed, "Don't you understand? I need to walk around!" (I was tempted to intercede several times but kept telling myself, "My pregnant wife is certainly going to get more sympathy than I am.") Finally, after more of Lori's pleading, the officer angrily shot back, "Fine, walk around!" (We teach people to watch out for the progression of emotions from first to fifth gear. He accelerated through all five, without a clutch, in a matter of seconds.)

I felt frustrated, knowing my wife well enough to realize she simply wanted to walk around to breathe calmly and ease her physical discomfort, mostly so the kids wouldn't see her losing control. She walked just far enough away that she was out of the kids' view and sat on the curb to settle down. (Meanwhile, the officer wrote out a major ticket.) Just watching what Lori was going through upset me further. I was pretty sure she wasn't going into labor, didn't need an ambulance, and would be okay if given time to unwind. (And I was getting aggravated about the ticket.) Finally, I knew I could no longer keep myself from getting involved . . .

This was clearly a situational disaster. One party acted, reflexively but perhaps not wisely. The other person overreacted to the first action. That overreaction fueled the first party to further over-react. Overreaction fueled overreaction. Escalation escalated to more escalation. Temperatures rose. Tempers flared. Babies cried. Stomachs churned. Egos inflated. Gauntlets were thrown. Until a tiny incident became a cause célèbre . . . Over what? A one-way street? A parking ticket? A woman in labor? Now Mark goes on to reveal the outcome of their seemingly disastrous situation. Not to give away the ending, but thanks to an eleventh-hour usage of N.I.C.E., Mark and Lori did not serve jail time.

## CLOSE ENCOUNTERS OF THE POLICE KIND
### Part II: Jail, Ambulance, or Plea Bargain

The first thing I did was try to neutralize my own emotions. I knew if I went after this police officer with a "See what you've done! How could you treat a pregnant woman like this?" approach, it would backfire. So I took a few deep breaths and called over a second officer who'd been watching the entire scene. I said, "Could you do me a favor and sit and watch my kids in the car so that I can go talk to the other officer?" He obliged. I walked over to the original officer and very calmly said, "Look, I'm really sorry about all this. I know we were in the wrong and we accept that, but I really don't think we need the ambulance right now. I think if I just take my wife home, she'll be okay." At that point, I felt pretty good about how reasonable I sounded. But the officer slapped the ticket in my hand and exploded, "No, sir! She told me she was going into labor. I must get the ambulance." I stayed (relatively) calm and pursued my point. "But, Officer, we really don't need it. Let's just resolve the situation." Just as I was complimenting myself on being Mr. Cool, the officer blasted back, "Listen, you just get back to your car and your kids. If you're a good father, you'll get back to your kids!" *If I'm a good father . . . If? . . . If? . . .* It was like a sharp stick in my otherwise unbatting eye, a jab at my parenting skills, a challenge to my manhood.

I could sense my neutralization of emotions deneutralizing. I could feel meltdown coming. But again, I stopped myself. After all, I teach dealing with these types for a living. I thought to myself, "This guy is either a bully or is just doing this because he's always done this." I decided that what I needed to do was step away, physically and figuratively. I would try to talk to the other officer, the nice one who was watching the kids. I formulated my strategy, a solution composed of two options: (1) "We'll wait for the ambulance, but you must understand that since my wife feels it is unnecessary, she may not get into it" and (2) "Let us go now and we'll take the ticket and be on our way."

Strategy in mind, I approached the officer who was watching the kids, intending to say, "You're not caught up in the situation. Can we talk about it?" But before I could say anything, the officer preempted me, "If you were a good husband, you'd be concerned about your wife and not just getting out of here." Now I had two officers assailing my fatherhood and husbandhood.

As I turned to face off with the original officer, I could feel my own emotions ratcheting up. I was ready to stick my finger in his face and tell him my husbanding and fathering were none of his official police business when I finally realized this simple, unfortunate situation was escalating out of control, way out of control. I stopped myself then and there. It was my turn to take a deep breath. Just as we teach, I counted to ten, slowly. I went over to my wife and told her, "I'll be with the kids. Just relax, everything's going to be okay." She nodded and said she was fine.

I went back to my kids, settled them down, and, ticket in hand, quietly waited for the ambulance. It arrived; the EMTs checked Lori and pronounced her okay and not in labor, and, with the officer's blessing, the ambulance drove off *without* Lori in the back. Having long since missed the end of the game and Run the Bases Day, we were ready to head for home. As we pulled out of our (illegally gotten) parking space, the same, previously irrational, arbitrary, unsympathetic police officer stopped all traffic to make sure we could exit safely, escorted us out to the main road, waved goodbye, and wished us well. He could have been the star of a recruitment video for polite police . . . once the offending circumstances were over.

What I realized afterward is that he had been caught in a bad situation and had reacted to that situation rather than responding particularly and sensitively to the specific realities confronting him. He was conditioned to react and he did.

Here was the situation: A woman was breaking the law by driving past a Do Not Enter sign. She could not produce a registration for her car. She claimed she was going into labor. He then reacted by writing a ticket, writing a second ticket, calling my wife on her scam to get out of the ticket, and calling an ambulance (to avoid a lawsuit in the event she wasn't scamming).

He was locked into a certain pattern of behavior and couldn't break his training. Of course, if he had said, "Look, I have to call an ambulance as a matter of procedure, to prevent legal action,"

I'd have been much more understanding. But he didn't. He continued to escalate his emotions, which escalated Lori's, which escalated mine, and his, and the other officer's, and mine again.

The real lesson from the story is this: If I had allowed my emotions to go where they were headed, if I hadn't realized that this was a situation where it was best to "end without escalating," it could have escalated into a true nightmare. I'd have stuck my finger in the officer's face; he'd have arrested me (in front of my kids), put me in the back of his cruiser, put my wife in the back of an ambulance (without her husband), written us not one but two tickets, and delivered my children to the custody of their aunt and uncle until their mother got over false labor or their father was released on bail from jail.

This was a classic Situationally Difficult encounter. Once the situation changed, so did the behavior. The bad cop became the good cop. The key was identifying the type. Not doing so could have meant disaster.

So how can you make sure you know you're in a Situationally Difficult situation? Try the following exercise to see.

## EXERCISE: SITUATIONAL CLUE SPOTTING

Go back and reread the story as a detective searching for behavioral clues that suggest situational perpetrators: an action or reaction, physical or verbal, a word or retort, body language, a challenging remark, a defensive comeback, a heated exchange, an escalation. Look for the progression from mild pressure to medium pressure to a real pressure-cooker situation.

Put a checkmark next to each clue that signals stress or reaction to stress. Now imagine doing that next time you're face-to-face with someone who seems to be overreacting to the circumstances at hand. Put little imaginary checks in your mental margins. Try to do it not only for the other person but for yourself if you feel you might be reacting to the negative situation.

Spotting the problem is half the battle. At least you can stop yourself if not the other person. For more methods on counteracting the Situationally Difficult, see Chapter 11.

## HIGH-STAKES SITUATIONAL DIFFICULTIES

In case you think situational difficulties are largely harmless annoyances—life's little inconveniences, not life-threatening encounters—consider the following incident that occurred in the heat of the search for the D.C. sniper in 2002. It makes Mark and Lori's Run the Bases Day problems pale by comparison.

## GRANDMA AND GRANDPA, THE D.C. SNIPER SUSPECTS

An older couple—husband and wife antiques dealers and grandparents—were pulled over and surrounded by state troopers while driving from Maryland to Delaware. The troopers then called in F.B.I. agents who frisked, interrogated, and detained the couple for several hours, all because their vehicle roughly matched the police alert for "a white box truck with a dent or white van." To say the authorities were situationally wrought up would be drastic understatement. After all, the mid-Atlantic area was living in daily fear of the next sniper shooting. To the couple's credit, they recognized the tension and stress citizens and authorities were under and managed to remain calm and cooperative even as the police and F.B.I. treated them like hardened criminals. Their composed behavior definitely defused the situational difficulty more quickly than confrontational behavior would have.

Even the most controlled among us would have had a hard time maintaining such calm. However, it's important to remember that understanding circumstances can be the key to resolving an inflammatory circumstance.

# CHAPTER NINE

# The Photo Shop Clerk

*Dealing with the Strategically Difficult*

## YOU'RE READY FOR STRATEGICALLY DIFFICULT

W E HAVE a virtually foolproof method of determining if we're dealing with a Strategically Difficult person, our Strategic Suspect Checklist. If you can answer yes to any of these, you're facing a strategic challenger.

- ✓ They make you feel as if they're "up to something." Trust your gut. If you feel it, you're not paranoid; you've got good instincts.
- ✓ They try to convince you (by persuasion or by mandate) that you must play by their rules.
- ✓ They will modify (not abandon, but within the bounds of strategy) their behavior if properly handled. (How-to tips come later in the chapter.)

## THE HIGHLY EFFECTIVE TACTICS OF STRATEGICALLY DIFFICULT PEOPLE

These are the Top Twenty Tactics employed by Strategically Difficult people. Strategically Difficult people are, by definition, employers of strategies composed of calculated and practiced tactics. By observation, comparison, research, and collected painful real-life stories, we've assembled and categorized them to help you spot them, label them, and prepare to deal with them. Almost any tactic you will come across is, in some way, a variation on one of these "greatest hits."

Read through the list and you will, no doubt, recognize methods or versions of methods you've faced. As you do, you may note that these tactics are not the exclusive province of Strategically Difficult types. They're often used by Situationally and Simply Difficult types as well. We ascribe them mostly to Strategically Difficult people because they are most analytical in their application of tactics, but don't be surprised if any and all types of B.T.I.P. use them. Be prepared to spot them and to counter them. Later on, we will provide you with powerful countertactics for effectively dealing with these strategies, regardless of which type is employing them.

## THE TOP TWENTY TACTICS OF STRATEGICALLY (AND SOMETIMES SITUATIONALLY OR SIMPLY) DIFFICULT PEOPLE

1. *Higher Authority*—Once a final decision is agreed upon (or seems to be agreed upon), the other side claims he or she lacks the power to make the decision really final or official.

2. *Good Cop/Bad Cop*—Two people are involved on the other side in a deal or negotiation. One acts like your advocate or ally while the other acts like your adversary, manipulating you the entire time.

3. *Take It or Leave It*—This is the no-negotiation posture of "My first offer is my final offer."

4. *False Deadlines*—The other side creates an arbitrary time pressure (that seems real) in order to try and make you come to an agreement that may not be ideal.

5. *Passive-Aggressive*—In the midst of "dealing," the other person will stop dealing and shut down. It is a seeming sabotage of the deal with inaction, again aimed at getting you to accept less-than-optimal terms.

6. *The Wince*—You make an offer and the other person reacts with an exaggerated facial expression to get you to question the reasonableness of your offer. His face seems to say, "Oh my God, you must be kidding!" or "You're out of your mind!"

7. *Silence*—The other person simply creates ominous "dead space" that may intimidate you into disclosing important information or even capitulating on a key point.

8. *The Red Herring*—The other side focuses on unimportant details (acting as if they are important) in order to divert attention from the real deal points.

9. *Outrageous Behavior*—The person on the other side is given to sudden, loud outbursts or other socially errant behavior—again, to take focus off of the real issues.

10. *Nibbling*—The deal seems to be set. Then the other side makes a small (so it seems) addition at the eleventh hour. Then another small addition. And another.

11. *Physical Surroundings*—The other side controls a venue to gain an advantage, such as controlling your comfort level, location, resources, and so on.

12. *Ganging Up*—You are dealing one on one with another person. Without warning, he or she brings someone else to the bargaining table. You are outnumbered and possibly outflanked by expertise or rank.

13. *Surprise Information*—After exploring a potential deal and supposedly putting all relevant data on the table, the other side introduces new information, catching you off guard and unprepared.

14. *Trust Me*—The other person tries to force concessions from you with fantasy promises of making it up to you in some future but indeterminate deal.

15. *Smoke Screen*—A strategy of planned obfuscation, the other side deliberately confuses the issues, facts, and figures so that you lose track of key elements or, by the time you return to them, are less intent on their exact definitions.

16. *Denial*—The other side simply denies having agreed to a point that had clearly been agreed upon earlier, in order to reopen it and win back the point.

17. *The Bluff*—The other side tells you something that may or may not be true, yet you are suspicious.

18. *Controlling the Contract*—The other side drafts the contract after agreement and, to your detriment, makes changes to which you had not agreed, usually to gain an advantage after you think the deal is done.

19. *Withdrawal*—The other side, suddenly and precipitously, retracts a proposal so as to force hurried acceptance.

20. *Monetary Concessions*—These are sneaky pleas or suggestions by your adversary to get you to reveal your price and/or lower your price, so that he can hold you to that number and convince you that you made an offer.

So you can better identify these tactics when used against you, and to understand the context in which each is used, we have constructed the Tactic Deactivator, which you'll find in Chapter 12.

We encourage you to consult the Tactic Deactivator to learn the identifying characteristics of these tactics as well as conceptualize the scenarios in which you will commonly find them.

## EXERCISE: COUNTERTACTICS— THE FREQUENT FIVE AND THE FEARED FIVE

Here's a simple exercise in preparing for Strategically Difficult people (or anyone who happens to employ a strategic tactic). Go back to the list and check off the five tactics you encounter most frequently. Then check off the five you find most challenging or fearful. Now look at your Frequent Five and your Feared Five. Think about how you deal with the Frequent Five, the methods you use and the countertactics you employ. Look at the Feared Five and see if your methods apply. If not, in the absence of pressure of the moment, think of what tactics might work for you. The first step to dealing with B.T.I.P. is being prepared for their acting like B.T.I.P.

Before discussing the countermeasures to control a situation created by the tactic-wielding, Strategically Difficult person, let's take a look at how to spot those tactics.

Here's another story from Mark's real-life adventures, this one involving an immovable object, a Strategically Difficult store clerk, and a relentlessly determined force, Mark himself. As in the case of the Situationally Difficult story, Mark retells this one in two parts. The first part provides a graphic illustration of how rigid and unrelenting a strategic foe can be. As a result, is this strategic encounter a lost cause? You'll see in the second part, which reveals the outcome (page 103). In both parts, we've noted the presence of various forms of some of the Top Twenty Tactics.

## THE PHOTO SHOP CLERK
### *Part I: What Part of "No" Don't You Understand?*

I have a gang of ten friends that goes back a long way with a lot of colorful history. Every year we get together for our annual "adrenaline rush" adventure—from skydiving to swimming with sharks to bungee jumping or playing paintball—anything that's a little bit dangerous and maybe less than mature as we get older. But to us, these are special, if not sacred, rituals.

One day I got an invitation to a party that would be a rare opportunity to see the whole crew. Not long before, I had had a roll of film developed that had a great shot of all ten of us from our last hair-raising adventure. How great would it be to get copies made and pass them out to the other nine at the party! I put the original photo in my car to remind myself to get the copies made the next chance I had. Being the procrastinator I am, getting those copies didn't occur to me again until the evening I was driving to the party.

On the way, I saw a one-hour photo shop and, never believing it's too late for anything, pulled in. If they had one of those machines that make color photo reprints on the spot, maybe I could get the copies in the next hour. Or, ever the optimist, maybe I could even talk them into shortening the one hour to a half hour . . . or fifteen minutes.

Photo in hand, I announced to the clerk, "I want nine copies of this picture. How much will that be?" She responded, "Ninety dollars." I responded (perhaps too bluntly) to her response, "That's ridiculous." She just pointed to an official store sign on the wall reading, "Reprints $10 Each" (Tactic 1—Higher Authority). Then, like a grade-school teacher, she did the math. "Nine times ten is ninety dollars. If you want the pictures, that's the price" (Tactic 3—Take It or Leave It).

I wanted the copies for my friends, but the price of friendship was getting pretty high. I tried an angle that might help lower the cost. "Okay, let me ask you a question. Is there any way I can get a discount because I'm buying nine of them?" She didn't consider, ponder, cogitate, or hesitate. She said, "No." Just plain no. She did not raise her voice or try to explain herself (Tactic 5—Passive-Aggressive). I was amazed. Worse, I was losing my battle for the photos.

But I was self-aware enough to think, "This is the kind of circumstance that can fuel your emotions and exasperate you." I needed to identify what *type* of individual I was facing so I could determine *how* to deal with her. It was pretty clear that she was acting Strategically Difficult; that is, she was following "higher authority" rules given to her with her job. It provided her the strategy for virtually all issues. When in doubt, turn to the rules: The price is $x$, and 10 items $= 10 \times x$. Are there exceptions? No. Are there discounts? No. Are there any circumstances under which the price is different? No. If I was right and she was a Strategically Difficult person, she only had the authority to say no and lacked the authority to say yes.

There was only one way to find out. Come up with some options and see how she responded. I said, "All right, what if I offered to pay, say, fifty dollars for the nine copies?" Before I could even finish my sentence, she shot back, "You must be crazy! I told you, the price is ninety dollars!" (Tactic 6—The Wince).

I then said to her, "Think about this. If I can't do nine for fifty dollars, I'm only going to get one copy made. Would you rather make a fifty-dollar sale or a ten-dollar sale?" She stuck to the script. "I really don't care what size sale I make" (more of Tactic 3—Take It or Leave It).

I even tried to suggest there might be a career reward in it for her. "Tomorrow, you could tell your boss you made a fifty-dollar sale. Don't you care about that?" She didn't stray from her rote strategy, instead just stared at me without uttering a word for what seemed like several minutes (Tactic 7—Silence). She wasn't going to budge or blink. Getting a bit agitated, I asked, "Is your manager here?" She answered, "No, I'm afraid he isn't" (a variation on Tactic 1—Higher Authority).

Fine. If she's regurgitating the *Comprehensive Employee Manual of Customer Relations* (which has no doubt categorized and answered every imaginable problem), I'll just find out what the canned solution to my problem is, probably Section 116 C—Customer Feels Price Is Unwarranted. I'll let her solve the problem the way she was taught during employee training month (or week or minute).

I laid out the challenge. "I need to have nine copies of the same photo. I feel ninety dollars is more than what nine copies are worth. What can you do to help me out?" It took her a nanosecond to reply, "Nothing. We close in ten minutes and I don't even know if I can make nine copies before we close" (a variation on Tactic 19—Withdrawal).

No matter how creative my options, no matter how compelling my logic, no matter whether I was nice or not so nice, she remained steadfastly Strategically Difficult. Nothing worked. I was ready to give up. I thought, I'll get one extra copy and pass it around at the party. So what if my friends whisper that Mark is so cheap he only made one copy. "I'll just take one." She said, "Fine," took the photo over to the machine to run it through, and that's when it hit me. "Wait!" I bellowed, stopping her in her tracks and draining the blood from her face . . .

Okay, let's take inventory on what had occurred. Mark had run into a classic example of a Strategically Difficult person. It's interesting to note that despite the sophisticated sound of the label Strategically Difficult, the individuals you encounter may be average, smart, brilliant, clever, diabolical, or frequently, rotely robotic in their observance of strategy. They may be following their own self-created and modified strategy or, like the photo clerk, hewing to a strategy laid out for them by higher authorities, like soldiers following orders of superior officers. And like good soldiers, they'd rather die in action than disobey—which may be admirable in war but hardly helpful in practical, day-to-day encounters. In fact, the more rigid the adherence to strategy, the less independent the thinking you face, the more difficult you may find modifying the person's behavior. Witness that to this point, despite Mark's training and creativity, he had made no progress whatsoever. He had tried every imaginable way to get the clerk to change the rules. And therein lay the problem.

## THE PHOTO SHOP CLERK
### *Part II: Don't Break the Rules; Follow Them*

When she put my photo down on the copier, I realized it only took up about a third of the copy area of the screen. Excitedly, I suggested, "What if I laid three pictures down on the copy machine and we copied all three at once?" Having regained her color, and her impatience with me, she snarled, "I really don't care, sir. It costs ten dollars for a sheet of photo paper. We charge per sheet used, no matter what's on the copy." Great!

That meant if I copied the original three times, that would be thirty dollars, and then if I laid those three down and copied them on one sheet, that's another ten dollars, and then did that again, that's another ten dollars . . . and a total of nine copies for fifty dollars, a lot closer to what I had budgeted. She shrugged but didn't speak, which was her version of cooperation.

What I realized, as I waited for my copies (nine of them for fifty dollars!), was that I could have argued with this woman all night, used every form of rational persuasion available, ranted, raved, or begged, and I was never going to get anything but stock, strategic responses from her training manual. It was designed to handle all encounters—not necessarily well or individually, but simplistically, automatically, and requiring no thought whatsoever on the part of the employee. "This is the price. You buy or you don't. This is how long it takes. You either wait or you don't. This is our quality. You either like it or you don't. This is our guarantee. Read it. This is our return policy. Read it. These are our hours. Period. Etc., etc., etc. Without exception, variation, or modification."

"By the rules," she had to charge ten dollars per sheet of photo paper. Either the customer buys it or doesn't, period, without exception, variation, or modification. Only when I found a way to work within her strategy did I find an option that solved my problem.

As Mark's story demonstrates, and as we teach, in an odd way, the rules work. They have no gray area, only black or white. They constitute a total, immutable strategy. To utilize creative options, you must recognize and work *within* the particular strategy you face. By the way, it is unlikely that Mark's finding a creative option had any effect on the clerk's behavior with the next customer or the next challenge. She didn't process the encounter and say to herself, "You know, by listening to customer needs and trying to fulfill them, I will help the store do more business and maybe get a raise or promotion." She just reverted back to her strategy, "the rules," and recited them rigidly and obstinately until the customer either caved in, went away, or hung in there like Mark to find that elusive creative option.

---

# CHAPTER TEN

# The Boss from Hell
### *Dealing with the Simply Difficult*

## TAKE A DEEP BREATH AND GET READY FOR SIMPLY DIFFICULT

THERE'S DIFFICULT (situationally), more difficult (strategically), and then there's *really* difficult (simply). Simply doesn't mean simple or easy or run-of-the-mill. It means simply as in clearly, plainly, absolutely, totally, off-the-charts, without exception, all-the-time, over-the-top difficult. If you want to know for sure, refer to the following checklist. If the person you're dealing with matches these descriptions, he or she is a Simply Difficult person.

✓ *Irrationality as an art form.* They engage in behavior that is often irrational. They say what they want but not why. They demand but do not explain. They refuse to bargain or trade off. They seem determined to create lose-lose results.

✓ *Difficult rain or shine.* They are difficult regardless of the situation. In good times or bad times, when they have the advantage or lack it, when on their turf or yours, when they're getting their way or not.

✓ *No known cure.* They do not respond to attempts to de-escalate an encounter. Calming techniques do not calm.

Reason doesn't resound. Levity doesn't lift the negativity. They just keep ratcheting the tension higher and higher.

✓ *Famous (but not in a good way).* They have an established reputation for being very difficult. No matter whom you ask, you get the same answer (or grimace). They have few to zero fans or supporters and legions of victims.

## EXERCISE: THE SIMPLY DIFFICULT CHARACTERISTIC DETECTOR
### *(Or How to Know the Real Deal from the Imitation)*

Most nightmares are just bad dreams. When you're having them, they feel totally real. But then you wake up and realize things are not as bad as you imagined. The same is true for most difficult people you encounter. Eventually you realize they're not really as bad as you imagined. So be careful what or whom you label Simply Difficult. A Situationally Difficult person, in a particularly upsetting situation, can seem to be a true maniac, only to return to pretty reasonable behavior when the situation abates. And a Strategically Difficult person, utilizing a very rigid and unforgiving strategy, can seem to be a tyrant, until you crack the code of that strategy.

Before you conclude that someone actually is Simply Difficult, make sure you're not just living through a "nightmare," from which you'll awake relieved. To determine if your adversary is the real deal, ask yourself whether he or she exhibits the following traits:

Yelling, Shouting, and Screaming: *Berating as a means of communication, not just in the heat of the moment*
Scornfulness: *A willingness to ridicule you or others involved*

Absence of Sympathy: *Never showing a soft or vulnerable side, never revealing empathy, only self-absorption*

Egotism: *An unbridled self-interest and self-aggrandizement (note the recurrence of "self")*

Lack of Focus: *A jumping from topic to topic, from point to point, never settling one issue before leapfrogging to another*

Threats: *The constant use of intimidation, a willingness to destroy even their own gain to prevent yours*

Bullying: *Classic playground behavior, verbal pushing and shoving, and throwing power and weight around*

Duplicity: *Using lies as standard procedure tools*

Convenient Amnesia: *Not remembering promises or obligations, having no record of any deals or agreements (except those that are self-serving)*

*If* you find any or all of these characteristics and, most important, if they never subside, never disappear, never end, *if* the characteristics don't disappear when circumstances improve (Situationally Difficult), nor can they be blunted by a counterstrategy (Strategically Difficult), *if* they just occur, unabated, without warning, reason, or pattern until the person gets his or her way, *if* the unreasonable behavior is relentless . . . that's when you know, there's no waking up from this nightmare, that you are face-to-face with a Simply Difficult type.

## MAD DICTATORS DON'T JUST RUN COUNTRIES— SOMETIMES THEY RUN COMPANIES

What comes next is a story that involved both Ron and Mark. It concerns a woman who came to them for help when she was squaring off against a truly intimidating, card-carrying, no-holds-barred despotic Simply Difficult boss. Again, the story is told in two parts. In the first part you see the conduct that distinguished the boss as a Simply Difficult type, its effect on his victim, and her seeming powerlessness. Later, in the second part (page 114), we'll relate how she dealt with the boss.

## THE BOSS FROM HELL
### *Part I: High-Paid Abuse*

This story involves no one with great fame, wealth, or political power. It's the story of a woman who worked for a really terrible boss we'll call Ivan. Sound familiar? We've all had one, maybe not this bad . . . or maybe worse.

This woman—let's call her Virginia—was familiar with the methods we teach for dealing with difficult people. In fact, when we met, she calmly introduced herself and said, "I appreciate your 'nice' approach and I think it works in many, even most situations . . ." We knew a "but" couldn't be far behind. Her emotional level crept up ever so slightly. "But you don't understand." Her face began to flush, her tone heightened, and her voice trembled. "My boss is a nightmare. A true nightmare. A living horror. Hell on earth!" In the space of ten seconds, just describing him took her from composed to visibly shaken.

We asked her to tell us the whole story. Virginia tried to regain her composure as she recounted her daily misery. "No matter what I do, no matter how hard I try, no matter how patient I am, no matter how much I put up with, no matter how nice I am, it never, ever, ever works with this man." At this point, she literally stopped to catch her breath. Just observing the toll of telling her story, it was apparent what damage this boss had done. She went on, giving specific and graphic examples of his abuse. If Ivan missed a plane, he took her head off for not getting him out of the office in time. If a client was a no-show, he let loose a tirade for screwing up his appointments. If he bid on a contract and didn't get it, he yelled, screamed, and ranted that she'd written the wrong terms into the bid. If he was running late, he pounded the desk, kicked wastebaskets, and let out bloodcurdling shrieks two inches from her face that it was because she overscheduled him. If he forgot to return a call, he swore, cursed, and hollered at the top of his lungs that she'd never given him the message. Ivan belittled, berated, and ranted. He'd even thrown things at her. And he constantly threatened her with demotion or firing (Irrationality as an art form).

The obvious question was, why would she put up with him? Unfortunately, the answer was equally obvious. She needed the job. It paid well, very well, and as a result, it would be hard to find commensurate income elsewhere. And the boss, terrible Ivan, knew it. So she accepted what amounted to battle pay. He felt he had bought the right to abuse her.

Her story was reminiscent of a famous anecdote about the executives who worked for the infamous banking baron J. P. Morgan (though the apocryphal story has been attributed to countless other ruthless bosses). Morgan was tyrannical. He demanded endless, thankless work from his cadre of distinguished, educated, highly skilled business managers. He was notorious for never complimenting, but always disparaging their efforts, privately and publicly. But he paid them huge sums of money. When asked why these men continued to work for the abusive Morgan, one replied, "He's got us by our limousines."

Like his minions, Virginia said she felt trapped, wanting to escape but held hostage by the money. There was hardly an easy solution to this one. Nonetheless, we sat with her to plot out a course of action.

We should note, up to this point, she had done a pretty good job of trying to neutralize her emotions. Certainly, she revealed her sensitivities as she recounted her plight, but she remained rational and analytical throughout. And, to date, she had held her feelings in check at work, continuing to do her job even under the most adverse conditions. We walked her through our identification process. Perhaps he was Situationally Difficult. She told us she had tried to defuse negative situations, waited for them to pass, or offered sympathy. He rejected her overtures and redoubled his odious behavior. And when she waited for a negative situation to pass, it never did, or was replaced by another and another negative circumstance. If it was an unpleasant situation, it was a lifelong one (Difficult rain or shine). So much for the boss being Situationally Difficult and attributing his behavior to a "bad day."

We then considered that he might be Strategically Difficult. We talked about tactics he had used and how she'd dealt with them. Fortunately, she had done a pretty good job of identifying and attempting to overcome these actions, but his behavior had not changed a bit. Rather than even consider her responses to his tactics, Ivan shut them down summarily (No known cure). Behavior that never de-escalates, even when it appears tactical, usually is a sign of someone worse—a Simply Difficult person.

When we added up the characteristics, he created an almost perfect profile of the Simply Difficult individual. We then put her boss to the last test. Did he have a "reputation" for being Simply Difficult? Was he willing to shoot himself in his own foot just to make sure he inflicted pain on others? She described to us just such a person. Not only was he abusive to her, but he had acted in the same uncivilized manner toward her predecessors in the job. He was rude and offensive to others in the office. Even clients were treated to his crude transgressions. More than once he fired his most capable salespeople (and hurt the company's sales) just because he felt they were getting "too big for their britches." Hurting the company (and presumably his own paycheck) was worth it to him just to "teach someone a lesson." Unfortunately, he was definitely and without a doubt a Simply Difficult person (Famous, but not in a good way).

The terrible boss in this story is a classic. He displayed not one or two, but all four of the characteristic traits on our checklist for the Simply Difficult type. Look at the following excerpts from the story and note how each offered irrefutable evidence to label this man Simply Difficult:

No matter what I do, no matter how hard I try, no matter how patient I am, no matter how much I put up with, no matter how nice I am, it never, ever, ever works with this man (Textbook description of an individual who does not respond to attempts to de-escalate encounters).

If Ivan missed a plane, he took her head off for not getting him out of the office in time. If a client was a no-show, he unleashed a tirade on her for screwing up his appointments. If he bid on a contract and didn't get it, he yelled, screamed, and ranted that she'd written the wrong terms into the bid. If he was running late, he pounded the desk, kicked wastebaskets, and let out bloodcurdling shrieks inches from her face that it was because she overscheduled him. If he forgot to return a call, he swore, cursed, and hollered at the top of his lungs that she'd never given him the message. Ivan belittled, berated, and ranted. He'd even thrown things at her. And he constantly threatened her with demotion or firing (Several examples of displays of irrational behavior).

He rejected her overtures and redoubled his odious behavior. And when she waited for the negative situation to pass, it never did or was replaced by another and another negative circumstance . . .

Rather than even consider her responses to his tactics, Ivan shut them down summarily (More and more clues of being Simply Difficult regardless of the situation).

Not only was he abusive to her, but he had acted in the same uncivilized manner toward her predecessors in the job. He was rude and offensive to others in the office. Even clients were treated to his crude transgressions (Confirmation of his reputation for being Simply Difficult).

The identification was complete, and as uncomfortable as her circumstances were, at least she knew exactly what she was dealing with. The conclusion might have been that she could do nothing about him. Perhaps the best approach would be to accept the reality and walk away from terminally unpleasant circumstances. Before taking that route, we both thought it was worth more pursuit. We coached this woman through an approach that *just might* work, even on Ivan the Terrible. We gave her a crash course in shaping a solution called balancing the power, which we'll explain in detail later. But first, Mark tells the conclusion to her horror story.

## THE BOSS FROM HELL
### *Part II: Oh Yeah?!*

What could she do? We asked Virginia, "What have you done to balance the power?" She couldn't even fathom that she had a shred of power, let alone enough to balance his. She said, "How can I possibly balance the power? I work for him. He's my boss. He reminds me all the time. I'm just an assistant. I'm powerless."

We explained that Simply Difficult people are bullies because they believe, and often the rest of us accept, that they have power to bully.

In fact, people only have power if we give it to them. And we always have some power of our own. What power did she have? We told her that together we were going to look for her power, assuring her that it did exist. We would find it, assess it, and determine how best to use it.

First, we established that if she thought she had no option but to work for Ivan, she was granting him huge clout. On the other hand, if she was open to the idea that there might be other employment alternatives out there, she was taking back a good deal of his leverage and creating her own power.

The first step was for Virginia to search out other work opportunities, careers and jobs she would find interesting and rewarding. She did and came back with a report that didn't surprise us. With her skills, a number of jobs surfaced. However, not one of them paid as well as her current job. She even lamented the fact that some were quite appealing but she simply couldn't afford to take them. We pushed her a bit further on this point.

We asked, "Is the amount of abuse you are suffering worth the extra dollars?" We wanted her to think of it that coldly, in terms of the amount of abuse a dollar could purchase. When she was forced to evaluate it that way, she answered, "No, it's not worth it. I would rather make less and be happier." That was a major step forward in gaining power. She then rethought her priorities—bills, savings, necessities, and luxuries—and found a way to budget her life on a lower income. That really changed the power balance, because now she had a "walkaway position."

Of course, it didn't fully balance the power, so next we performed an audit of her value in the equation. "Realistically, what would happen if you left?" As she contemplated that scenario, for the first time in our dealings, she laughed. She recalled the horror stories she'd heard from office veterans about her predecessors, none of whom had lasted more than six months. She was considered something of a marvel, having survived six years. We asked, "What happened in the past when he lost each of those assistants?" Virginia replied with a detailed account. "They say it was chaos. Ivan's assistants arranged all of his appointments, phone calls, planes, trains, hotels, dinners, family matters, gifts, cards, you name it. If he didn't have someone to do those things, his life became a shambles. He skipped appointments, didn't return calls, missed planes and trains, didn't show up for dinners, forgot his own kids' birthdays, and went berserk over every screwup. I believe it because I book his life, literally, every hour of every day."

"So," we asked, "what would happen if you weren't there?" A look of recognition came over her as if she had just learned a big secret. Without her, his life would be a shambles again. Turmoil. Chaos. Nightmare. Disaster. We looked at her and smiled. "You have real power."

She had never looked at it that way. She always saw it as boss-assistant, Ivan-Virginia, czar-serf. Ivan had all the chips in the card game. But once we planted the idea that she had alternatives—the possibility of walking away and power of her own—she realized that she was in a position to confront him and the issue directly.

Her next step was a face-to-face conversation. With all of the rational reassurance on her side, she was still plenty intimidated by the prospect of a showdown. As she reported later, she walked in that day looking confident but feeling terrified inside. That's okay; in fact, it's normal. After all, you are trying to balance power that has been tipped one way for years. You have every right to feel queasy.

On D-day, inside his office, she had decided to go about their normal business until the moment he reverted to his vile behavior. As expected, it didn't take long. He began to unleash a classic tirade.

*Ivan:* Where are my expense reports? Did you lose them? You did, didn't you?

*Virginia:* I put them on your desk first thing this morning.

*Ivan:* Well, they're gone now! You must have thrown them out in one of your cleaning frenzies!

*Virginia:* I put them on your desk after I straightened it.

*Ivan:* They're gone! Just admit it! Now you'll have to reconstruct my expenses from the last month because you've screwed up again!

*Virginia:* The reports are under your briefcase.

*Ivan:* Who the hell put my briefcase on top of the reports? I sure didn't!

*Virginia:* I don't know. It's your briefcase.

*Ivan:* Don't tell me what I did!

At that point, instead of taking any more, she stood up, looked across the desk at him, and said, "Stop. You will no longer treat me like this." She said she was shaking inside but must have sounded confident because the boss looked stunned. She had never stood up to him in the past. She kept going. "I have looked for other opportunities. I admit they don't pay as well, but I've decided my dignity and happiness are more important than money. Unless you agree to the following terms, I am prepared to walk out this door this minute." She said he was silent, for one of the few times in his life. She kept rolling. "You will no longer abuse me verbally. You will not yell or curse at me. You will no longer call me and demand work at inappropriate times. You will not embarrass me in front of other workers. You will show me the respect I have earned."

By this time the boss had regained his composure and his voice. To say he was upset would be an understatement. He countered, "How can you treat me this way? You're being ridiculous. Sit down and get back to work."

Without another word, she turned and walked toward the door. He called after her, "What are you doing?" She said, "I told you what my terms are. If you can't agree to them, I'm leaving. Good luck." He jumped out of his chair and stopped her at the door, begging, "I can't have you leave." She said, "Then you have to start treating me with the professional dignity I have earned."

He looked at her, swallowed hard, and said, "I'm sorry." (She told us later that those were words she thought she'd never hear him say to anyone, least of all to her.) He went on, "I know I'm difficult to deal with. I apologize. I will try."

By this time her confidence was high. She didn't just accept his promise. She looked him in the eye and said, "You have to do more than try. You have to really do it. Because if you don't I will walk out of here—happily ever after."

When she reported the story back to us, she had put in several weeks with the "new" boss—the less difficult, more reasonable, more respectful boss. She said he was not only trying; he was doing it. Of course, he still had moments when his temper would flare and he'd have to stop himself in midcurse. She could see his lip curl and his forehead wrinkle and his face turn red, but he stopped himself before the epithets escaped. He wasn't perfect, but he was better.

Another month later, he hadn't reverted to his old self. Evidently, he had really believed she would walk out. He had seen the balance of power shift from being all his to an offset on her side. He realized he had a lot to lose if he lost her. So he did what he could to de-escalate himself from a Simply Difficult to one who was merely difficult.

She is now approaching her seventh year working for him, another record. As for the other people in and out of the office, he still abuses them. They haven't balanced the power—yet.

Regardless of how lopsided the power distribution may appear or how powerless you may feel or how powerful your adversary seems to be, regardless of how unbalanced you may think the balance is, you have more power than you think. It's just a matter of finding your strength and the opposition's vulnerability. Think of the old joke about the woman who goes to the dentist for a root canal treatment. Just as the dentist is about to put the whirring drill into her tooth, she reaches up and grabs him by a delicate part of his anatomy. As he gasps for breath, she says, "Doctor, we're not going to hurt each other, are we?" That's balancing the power.

Okay, you know the three types of animal in the difficult

species and you know how to spot them in their natural environments or pick them out of a lineup of difficult suspects. Now all you have to learn is how to make each one behave better. No small task but absolutely an attainable goal. How to tame the B.T.I.P. is what comes next.

## PART FOUR

# C—Control the Encounter

*Shaping the Outcome*

# CHAPTER ELEVEN

# First-Class Treatment Gets a First-Class Upgrade to the Hall of Fame

*Controlling the Encounter with the Situationally Difficult*

## I KNOW THE TYPE—NOW WHAT?

Now THAT YOU KNOW who, or what, you're facing, what can you do about him, her, or them? Unfortunately, you can't just say, "Hey, you're being Situationally Difficult. Cut it out!" Or "I know you. You're Simply Difficult. It won't work on me." Real life doesn't play out like a television show when the wise and thoughtful person has a heart-to-heart talk with the insensitive, badly behaved person as dramatic music hits a crescendo and the previously bad person experiences an epiphany, a moment of "Ah-hah! I've been so wrong. It's time to change my ways." It just doesn't happen like that in everyday business or life, at least not very often.

## ONE SIZE DOES NOT FIT ALL

Instead, we run into people who are uncooperative or close-minded or implacable, and despite our best TV lectures, they stay that way. Then we find ourselves in a place called "stuck." Neither party gets anywhere and progress seems impossible. The key word is *seems*. Because more often than not, when dealing with difficult people, we try (unsuccessfully) to utilize the same methods we might with reasonable people, methods designed for people trying to find solutions rather than for people busy being difficult.

## SHAPING THE FACTORS THAT INFLUENCE, PERSUADE, AND DETERMINE OUTCOMES

We've already discussed the concept of neutralizing *your* emotions. That puts you in a position to rationally recognize what's happening in an encounter and not allow your own human reactions to create obstacles. You cannot, however, totally control the emotions of the other side. What you *can* do, though, is control the encounter and, as a result, shape, influence, and even determine the behavior of the other side, calming emotions if not controlling them.

Of the three types of difficult people, only the Situationally Difficult characteristically have their emotions running high. In fact, you cannot get a Situationally Difficult person to just rationally arrive at a sensible compromise until the situation itself is ameliorated (or at least acknowledged) and until his or her emotions are calmed. Once he, she, or they are calmed, then you can begin the process of controlling the encounter to achieve your desired outcome.

On the other hand, when it comes to Strategically Difficult or Simply Difficult types, neutralizing other people's emotions has little, if any, impact on controlling the encounter, controlling their behavior, and ultimately controlling the outcome. Yes, these people may act emotionally. They may be mad, sad, loud, inflammatory, or obnoxious. But dealing only, or even primarily, with their emotional symptoms will likely get you nowhere. There is much more behind their behavior than emotion. You cannot expect that calming the emotions of a Strategically Difficult person will result in his abandoning a strategy of outrageous demands, because it is in fact a strategy, a planned approach that he thinks has always worked for him. Instead, you must demonstrate clearly that this time his "proven" tactics are not working. You will not just roll over as a result of his old tricks. In other words, you must begin to control the encounter in order to control or influence his behavior and, ultimately, the outcome.

Be forewarned: Do not delude yourself (and set yourself up for unbridled abuse) by thinking the Simply Difficult person will let you deal with, influence, or even talk about (let alone calm) his or her emotions. Simply Difficult people do not act emotionally; they *are* emotional beasts, to the core. This is part and parcel of their being. They are mad or wild or voracious or just out of control, through and through. A Simply Difficult person who is acting irrationally, destructively, and obstreperously is not suddenly going to become rational, constructive, and cooperative, no matter what emotion-neutralizing methods you employ—until you can begin demonstrating you have as much or more power than he or she does or you're willing to abandon the deal rather than make a bad one. Again, you must begin to control the encounter by showing that his or her methods are not going to work or by showing that you may walk in order to alter behavior and impact the final results.

There are specific techniques of controlling the encounter that work for each type of difficult person. Of course, first you must determine the type of difficult person you face and then select the most effective response. Then it can be refined and adjusted to the specifics of the particular individual and conditions. Always remember that before you jump to solutions, you have to control the encounter. That means assessing the opposition's techniques and behavior, sending clear messages about what is or isn't going to work on you and why, demonstrating a balance of power, and then beginning to shape the actions that follow. Once you begin to control the encounter, the other side will begin to work with you toward solutions.

The person opposite you is Situationally Difficult. Do you rationally explain your point of view? Forcefully take the bull by the horns and match him emotion for emotion? Analytically propose solutions and ignore his emotions? Reactively tell the person why his emotions are not appropriate? Meekly walk away and refuse to ever deal with that person again? Rarely will any of these solutions work with the Situationally Difficult, because despite their forthright nature, inherent in each is a fatal flaw.

Rational Responses: *Responding rationally falls on deaf ears when someone is being irrational. Irrational people cannot hear rationality over the din of their own illogic.*

Emotional Responses: *Matching emotion for emotion typically escalates problems rather than resolves them. Yelling begets yelling.*

Oblivious Responses: *Ignoring the emotions is like ignoring the huge elephant in the room. You may ignore it, but it's still there.*

Pedantic or Explanatory Responses: *Telling people emotions are not appropriate tends to fuel their fire. No one wants to hear, "Hey, stop acting crazy."*

Rejection Responses: *Walking away and refusing to deal with that person may at times be impossible and almost certainly will prevent resolution. It is, after all, rejection.*

When dealing with Situationally Difficult people, first focus on getting to the root of their situation—the circumstances that caused them to be emotional in the first place—before you attempt to respond. You must recognize the need to defuse their emotional state. This is the first step in controlling the encounter: By discovering the cause of emotions, you begin to neutralize (calm) their emotions, which allows you to address the real issues.

## THE GEARBOX OF EMOTIONS

As discussed earlier, Situationally Difficult people are, in general, reasonable individuals who become difficult to deal with as a result of stress, pressure, or events with a negative impact. Situationally Difficult people don't just flip like an on-off switch from nice to nasty in an instant (though it may feel like it). They actually accelerate, foot to the floor, ratcheting through their emotional gears, the red needle climbing from zero until it's pinned to the other side of the dial—from standstill to situationally reckless.

Picture the vehicle's acceleration, gear by gear, and you can parallel it to human behavior.

Neutral: *The person is calm and not yet involved in a situation that would warrant or cause him or her to become unpleasant.*

First Gear: *The person is presented with, or surrounded by, a situation (circumstance, change of conditions, challenge, news, etc.) that stimulates irritation, anxiety, nervousness, or tension.*

Third Gear: *By now, the situation has begun to escalate (either in reality or in the mind and emotions of the person affected). The person begins to turn tension to testiness, anxiety to anger, irritation to outrage.*

Fifth Gear: *If the person you're facing gets to fourth or fifth gear,*
*expect irrationality, outbursts, and behavior that defies logic.*
*At this point, it may be in your best interests to end, or*
*forestall, the interaction.*

But what happened to second and fourth gears? Just as a
NASCAR driver can skip gears when shifting in a race car, when
your emotions take over, you can fly past the usual interim steps.
Instead of recognizing the anxiety of first gear and having it build
at a normal, rational pace, phasing into second gear, Situationally
Difficult people will allow themselves and their emotions to shoot
right into the third gear of overreaction. Even worse, once having
reached anger and outrage, rather than experiencing another step
of seething buildup (i.e., fourth gear), they will fly right into out-
of-control, accident-waiting-to-happen fifth gear. (If it seems like
you hear awful noises as the Situationally Difficult person acceler-
ates wildly, it's the stripping of his emotional gears.)

Speaking of automotive analogies, here's a story—starring
you—that illustrates emotional gear shifting that can turn a neutral situation into a situational catastrophe.

## GUESS WHO I RAN INTO AT THE MALL . . .

You come out of the mall loaded with packages, pile them into the
back of your charming little Honda Civic (Hondas always seem
innocent, don't they?). You put your car in reverse, back out of your
space, and . . . smack into an oncoming monster of an SUV (they
make ideal bad guys, don't they?). Boom! SUV grille crushing cute
little Honda bumper. Crunch! Honda trunk folding like accor-

dion. Crackle! Headlights and taillights shattering. Klink! Klunk! Various pieces of Honda chrome hitting the ground.

You thought it was all clear when you glanced in your rearview mirror, but the other vehicle must have been coming down the parking lane pretty fast, because it appeared out of nowhere. You're not really sure the accident was your fault, but since you were the one backing up, you're prepared to apologize, exchange insurance info, maybe split the damages, or, if need be, even accept the full responsibility. You open your door in a most reasonable frame of mind when suddenly the SUV driver leaps out of his megatank, red-faced and ready for battle, shouting, "You idiot! Don't you look where you're going?"

Apology? Forget it. No way you're going to say you're sorry to this maniac. And why say you're sorry when you weren't wrong? You were right! You looked in the mirror before this lead-foot careened through like he was in Demolition Derby. He should apologize to you! He should pay for the damages! He should get a ticket! He should lose his license! And he shouldn't be driving that urban assault vehicle anyway!

See, you just went from neutral to fifth gear in a matter of seconds.

This kind of acceleration—the neutral-to-fifth-gear reaction—can occur anywhere, anytime, to anyone. Everything is fine one minute and suddenly one person goes from zero to light speed. And often it's contagious. One person's acceleration leads to, or feeds, another's. If it can happen at the mall parking lot, it can happen at the office or at home, in a staff meeting, or at the dinner table. It can happen while making a sales pitch, telling someone it's bedtime, brokering a deal on property, cutting the last piece of birthday cake, splitting account lists, or dividing house-hold duties. No encounter is immune to emotional escalation fever. So what's the cure?

You cannot problem-solve or even approach issues in third gear, let alone in fifth gear. Trying to take a Situationally Difficult person from fifth gear to first gear in one shift is only going to ruin someone's transmission. Instead, you must de-escalate or de-celerate and gradually return his or her behavior to neutral. Only then can you begin to develop options (more on options later) and problem-solve.

## COMMON GOALS, CLASHING METHODS

Consider the following observations based on our experiences in the financial services category; these lessons are illustrative of any number of business categories and personal situations—especially those that involve money. In financial services, two prevalent but often conflicting functions are salespeople and underwriters. While they share a common goal—to build the company's business—their methods and styles couldn't be more different. Sound famil-iar? Life is full of pairings of people or types who have common goals but seemingly opposite or conflicting styles or approaches: teachers and administrators, designers and engineers, architects and builders, and parents and children.

Our experiences over the years cover a wide variety of financial institutions, from local banks or savings and loans up to inter-national giants. No matter how big or small, no matter whether they're on the corner or on three continents, no matter how many zeros are attached to the deals, typically the relationship between salespeople and underwriters, or their equivalents, is strained. And the reason is simple: The salespeople have sales goals they're trying to meet—they want to close the deal—and the under-writers, on the other hand, are measured by their success only in placing the highest-grade financial transactions on the books. Salespeople see underwriters as traffic cops unreasonably holding them back from meeting their goals, while underwriters feel constant high-pressure heat from salespeople to "bend the rules." At the risk of generalizing, underwriters (and other parallel types) tend to be analytical problem solvers and salespeople tend to be more optimistic and driven by their passion for the "chase." In many situations, salespeople believe they are simply asking underwriters to approve "a perfectly good deal." The underwriters, being trained to be more realistic (or pessimistic by comparison to salespeople), immediately look for the potential problems with the deal. The optimistic salespeople, seeing the underwriters as inflexible and negative, become increasingly upset, as their disapproving counterparts deflate the salespeople's balloon.

Distressed, offended, and eventually exasperated by what they perceive as unreasonable people thwarting them from reaching their sales goals, salespeople become Situationally Difficult, shifting from first to third to fifth gear. Unfortunately, analytical underwriters may not identify these escalating emotions and simply propose seemingly rational "solutions," that is, criticism, alternatives, or wholesale changes to make the deal "okay." If the salespeople weren't already quite into fifth gear, this kind of "help" will surely put them there.

All communication breaks down. The underwriters, who are problem solvers by nature, immediately jumped to "solutions" (though they may be seen as deal sabotage to the salespeople). Even if the underwriter's solutions are perfect, until the salespeople's emotions are defused, even perfect solutions fall on deaf ears. Needless to say, otherwise helpful but imperfect solutions are also ignored and dismissed in the midst of the emotional firestorm of the salesperson. Many deals that could have gotten done fall apart because the underwriter and salesperson are unable to soothe and resolve escalating emotions.

In case the underwriters feel we are picking on them and blaming their side, it should be noted that the salespeople could also have prevented these breakdowns by following the first rule of N.I.C.E.—neutralizing their own emotions. If an individual—yes, even a passionate salesperson—is conditioned to look for signs of his or her own emotional intensification, he or she can spot it, arrest it, and begin to ratchet it down. And remember what we said up front, that there are endless parallel pairs of types throughout all aspects of life, people with common goals but conflicting methods of achieving them. The story that follows is an indelible example of just such a conflict that Mark and Ron encountered and, fortunately, were able to solve.

## IF WE'RE ON THE SAME SIDE,
## WHY ARE WE TRYING TO KILL EACH OTHER?

We were retained by First Union Bank (which has since merged with Wachovia) to maximize productivity within its commercial banking group, including both relationship managers (or salespeople) and underwriters. When we asked the group at large if they had any challenges involving internal negotiations, that is, with others in their company, one underwriter raised his hand and said, "I have a relationship manager that presses me constantly to bend the rules, and that pressure just makes me more resistant to approving his deals." We asked the underwriter if that relationship manager was still with the company. The underwriter fired an accusing finger out like an arrow and said, "Sure, he's sitting right there!"

As you can imagine, there was quite a stir of uncomfortable murmurs, but we quickly saw it was an opportunity to deal with, and learn from, the underwriter–relationship manager issue. After a few minutes of probing, we were able to determine that the relationship manager, not surprisingly, was an emotional type who would raise his voice, turn red, and flail his arms when things were not going his way. The relationship manager defended his actions, saying, "That's just my passion coming out." The detached, methodical underwriter, on the other hand, was uncomfortable with this "passion." It was at odds with everything the underwriter knew, believed in, and worshiped: logic, facts, and analysis. After more discussion, more exchange, and understanding of each other's training, orientation, and feelings, each recognized the need to be cognizant of what made the other tick . . . and good at his job.

Finally, the relationship manager committed to doing a better job of neutralizing his own emotions, if it meant that the underwriter would be more flexible when approving his deals. Instead of ripping through the gears, they both saw the advantage of reasoned communication. They both neutralized and could begin the process of controlling their next encounter. How they did it— or rather, how we facilitated their doing it—is with the technique described below.

## Lend an E.A.R. (to Downshift Emotions)

When emotions are at their height with a Situationally Difficult Person, nothing positive can happen. Even the best solution to a problem will fall on deaf ears. So how do you downshift emotions to the point that positive progress is possible? You, or the person you are dealing with, must hear a solution in order to consider it. You can open the other person's ears by using your E.A.R. Here's how it works:

**E**mpathize: *Let the other person know that you recognize that he or she is under emotional stress or pressure and that you've been in similarly difficult situations.*

**A**sk: *Take the time to ask a couple of nonthreatening questions to gain valuable information and to let the other person vent his or her emotions.*

**R**eassure: *Let the other person know that you believe, in time or with remedies, the situation will defuse and/or improve.*

Here's a very simple story that happened to Ron, but to which anyone who has traveled can relate. It is a minidrama of what can occur when someone is under pressure. Note how the application of each element of lending an E.A.R. served to alter the course of a situational conflict.

## FIRST-CLASS TREATMENT GETS A FIRST-CLASS UPGRADE . . . TO THE HALL OF FAME

In 2002 Eddie Murray was inducted into major league baseball's Hall of Fame. Eddie was one of my long-standing clients. I represented him in numerous contract negotiations, from player to manager, from team to team, and city to city. More important, over the years, he had come to be one of my closest friends. I wouldn't have missed his big day for anything. But . . . those of you who have had the privilege to visit Cooperstown, New York, know that this lovely town is, to put it mildly, not very accessible.

While I was looking forward to Eddie's induction ceremony, I was dreading the travel challenges I would have to surmount to get there. (Suffice it to say, Cooperstown doesn't have a major, or minor, airport.) And this trip came at the end of one of those weeks when it seemed as if I'd been traveling, or standing in lines, continuously, all day, every day, because in fact I had. I'd get up early to wait in line to get a seat assignment, wait in line to go through security, wait in line to board, then catch the very first flight out to one city, so I could arrive early enough to wait in line to get my boarding pass to catch the first connection to get to another city, and then wait in a cab line to get a taxi to go through morning rush-hour traffic to get me to a conference center in time to do a seminar. Then, once the seminar was finished, I'd reverse the process, going down to stand in the hotel cab line, catch a taxi during evening rush-hour traffic, race to the airport to check in, obtain a boarding pass, go back through security, a mirror image of the first half of my day. But, to any of you who commute as part of your jobs, I expect exactly zero sympathy. As they say, it goes with the territory.

Nonetheless, I would have to say, travel on the Hall of Fame induction day was a bad (and getting worse) version of a normally not-so-pleasant ordeal. My first flight had not only been late but very turbulent owing to a storm that was making its way east at the same time I was (if I were paranoid, I'd say the storm was following me). My flight was so late, I should have missed my connection, but the connection flight had been delayed too. When I got off the first delayed flight, I looked up at the arrival-and-departure screen and after each listed flight read "Canceled," "Canceled," "Canceled," interspersed with an occasional "Delayed." Outside, the sky was beginning to look a lot like Kansas in *The Wizard of Oz,* dark and ominous. Fortunately, I didn't see Toto flying through the air. I made my way to one of the day's many lines, this one at the airline check-in gate. People ahead of me and behind me in the line wore those unmistakable looks of weary, worn-out, riding-on-empty travelers. Suit creases had long since gone limp, starched shirts weren't, ties were pulled down and briefcases dragged, and salespeople's ever-present smiles were heading south. We could have all been extras in the classic Steve Martin–John Candy comic disaster movie *Planes, Trains, and Automobiles.*

By the time I made my way to the front of the line, I had observed a revealing pantomime between the gate agent and passenger after passenger. The traveler would present a ticket. The agent would look at it, furrow her brow, shake her head skeptically, glance at the clock, shrug pessimistically, then say something that clearly aggravated an already aggravated flier, and hand over a boarding pass. The agent would then grit her teeth, make a facial gesture that on a better day would've passed for a smile, and wave the next passenger/victim to the podium.

I stepped up for my turn, feeling like I was about to be sentenced by a hanging judge. And then it occurred to me. She wasn't the judge. She was a victim, like everyone else that day. She was one of us. Rather quietly I said, "Hi, I'm on the flight to Baltimore." She barely looked up as she replied, "Two other late incoming flights already missed their connections and we're trying to put those passengers on this flight, so it's oversold. The plane isn't even here yet. We don't know when it's getting here. And when it does get here, we don't know when it can take off in this weather." I nodded and handed her my ticket.

As she punched—and I do mean punched—my information into her computer, I saw that she looked even more weary and worn out than the travelers. We each had had a flight or two and a delay or two that day. She had had delays all day, flight after flight, with passenger after passenger trudging up to her gate, as bad weather turned worse, pushing each flight later and later. She faced every disgruntled traveler, each receiving bad news, each worn down by the day, each blaming her as she was, to them, the embodiment of the airline and, less logically, of the weather. She had tried to tame a herd of unpleasant, upset, free-range travelers that day. Now she looked as if she had used up every smile she'd been taught to deliver, including those in her reserve tank; she had run through every well-rehearsed answer, friendly sigh, and understanding nod in her training manual. I leaned over and said, "This kind of day must be awful for you. Traveling as much as I do, I can only imagine how difficult it is for you on these kinds of days." [*Empathize: Let the other person know that you recognize that he or she is under emotional stress or pressure.*] Her head tilted up to me, her face almost in shock. Clearly, none of the demanding, delayed, grounded, or rerouted passengers had even tried to see things from her perspective. She gave me a half-skeptical, half-hopeful look that translated to "Could he really care?" I went on, "How do you deal with all of these angry travelers?" [*Ask: Use nonthreatening questions to let the other person vent his or her emotions.*] She let down her emotional guard just a bit and her mood noticeably shifted as she explained, "Sometimes it's really hard. Sometimes I don't know what to do." I nodded in agreement. "Well, let's hope that tomorrow will be better and things can return to relative calm." [*Reassure: Let the other person know that you believe, in time or with remedies, the situation will defuse and/or improve.*]

The mere fact that I showed an interest and offered sympathy to her began to turn her from being (understandably) Situationally Difficult to a sympathetic fellow sufferer. She handed my ticket back and said, "I'll see what I can do."

A couple of hours, one soft pretzel, and two newspapers later, the connecting plane finally came in, unloaded, and began to re-board. As she called out the seating by row number, I heard my name called. "Will Mr. Ron Shapiro come to the podium?" It sounded like I was about to be chosen as a "volunteer" to get bumped from this oversold flight. I was so beat, I accepted my fate dutifully as I made my way to the counter. The gate agent handed me a first-class boarding card. "We're full in coach so we're moving a couple of people up to first. Have a good flight." I smiled. She smiled and offered me some of my own advice, "And if the flight is delayed getting off the ground, don't get upset. Try counting to ten." "Thanks," I said. "Have a better day tomorrow." Then she turned to her next task, steeling herself for the unpleasant task of announcing the names of those who hadn't made it onto this flight and would have to wait for the next one.

And I headed to Cooperstown, finally. They say that sometimes it takes a long time to get to the Hall of Fame, but it's worth the wait. They're right. It was a great day.

There are countless travel nightmares and surely they don't all end as well as Ron's did. In sharp contrast, we came across another traveler's tale, the one retold below. There was a running account in the various American City Business Journals (local market business publications) of a war of emotions and letters between a columnist and US Airways. In this case, at least one party, if not both, seemed *not* to be employing the empathetic methods of E.A.R. Moreover, both parties were willing to air their differences very publicly.

## CLOSED EARS, CLOSED MINDS

Jeffrey Gitomer, nationally syndicated columnist whose feature, "Sales Effectiveness," runs in the American Business Journals, had had a very unpleasant experience on US Airways. In a column entitled "Why Can't They Just Get Customer Service Right?" he recounted his incident in painfully vivid detail and extrapolated from it to a wholesale indictment of customer service in varied industries. Mr. Gitomer took readers through his own experience of travel hell and frustration and angrily took the airline's personnel and management to task for not delivering "customer service." He went on to attribute a good deal of the airline's recent troubles to their myopic view of customer needs. While he may have made valid points about the airline and other like businesses, he did so as an attack, rather than a constructive dialogue. In his ire, he did not empathize or take into account the airline's perceived reasons for "cutting costs" or services. He did not ask or conjecture as to why the airline (or other businesses) might be responding to economic pressures in ways he considered obviously flawed. And he certainly did not reassure by suggesting solutions that might address the airline's issues while simultaneously looking to customer needs. The response he got was not surprising. Shortly after his written diatribe was printed, a representative of the airline offered a rebuttal on the pages of the same publications.

US Airways executive Chris Chiames admitted that the airline is hardly perfect, that its staff is only human, and that mistakes are sometimes made in the area of customer service. But he did not really concede that Mr. Gitomer had made legitimate business points worth considering. Instead, he defensively went on to state that Mr. Gitomer's "verbal abuse of our employees is legendary and his tirades have left employees in tears." Chiames's written re-buke explains, "Mr. Gitomer's personal style and behavior tests the patience of even the most saintly of human beings . . . and our em-ployees are tired of his belligerence that is demeaning and unwar-ranted." While Chiames may well have been correct that Gitomer has been grossly impolite, he did not deal with the issues raised. Like Gitomer, he did not empathize, ask, or reassure. Instead, he just built a stone wall and defended.

Did anyone learn anything from this exchange? Did Mr. Gitomer change his style? Did he really consider the airline's plight? Did the airline treat customers differently? Did they weigh Gitomer's points? Did the two sides find any common ground? Did anyone use their E.A.R.s? No.

Our purpose in retelling this story is not to render a judgment as to who is right and who is wrong. Rather, it's to show how easily emotions can escalate and how not utilizing the tools to defuse emotions simply fuels further escalation, often reaching a point of no return.

## THE HOW-TO OF LENDING AN E.A.R.

When "lending an E.A.R.," it is not recommended that you take a rote or robotic approach and simply say, "I empathize with you. May I ask why you're so emotional? I reassure you it will get bet-ter." You are, after all, dealing with other human beings, not ro-bots. This mechanical and stiff approach will never work as well as one that is truly human and personal and reflects your own ap-proach as well as the needs of the person opposite you. There are significant ways you can adapt E.A.R. to suit your own style and, most important, be even more effective.

## USE THE "WITHOUTS"

There is a fine but critical line between understanding and capitulating. Understanding is just that—hearing, processing, and comprehending. Capitulating is equally clear—giving in, folding, surrendering. But it is not necessarily an either-or choice between the two. If you recognize the need to understand the other side so you know what you're up against, the demands made and why, the rewards and risks, and if you do not view understanding as defeat but rather as better arming your bargaining position, then you can utilize the tools of E.A.R. to achieve your goals. Instead of choosing between understanding and capitulating, use the delicate balance between the two. Use the "withouts." Understand *without* capitulating. Hear what is asked for *without* granting it. Comprehend why a demand is made *without* acquiescing.

### Empathizing Without Agreeing: *I Understand  Versus I Agree*
There is a fine line between empathizing and agreeing. By empathizing with someone, you are acknowledging that the other person is upset. By agreeing with them, you are telling them they are right. If you agree with them, it may only strengthen their resolve. If you empathize, you send a signal that you are not an adversary while maintaining the integrity of your position. The following are some common ways to empathize without agreeing:

> *"I can see why you would feel that . . ."*
> *"I am sure it is difficult to . . ."*
> *"I might feel the same way if . . ."*
> *"I know it's tough when you are dealing with . . ."*
> *"I would be upset too if . . ."*
> *"I can understand how challenging it is to . . ."*

There are many variations of the above statements, and the list is not meant to be exhaustive. When empathizing, what is most important is that you recognize that feelings and emotions have entered the situation. Starting the E.A.R. process with empathizing seems almost self-evident, yet many, even most, people do not do it. Watch others deal with Situationally Difficult people and you will see that empathizing is rarely the first thing they do. More often, they focus on the differences in position rather than the commonality of feelings. Then watch carefully when you begin to empathize with people who are being Situationally Difficult. The surprised look in their eyes, followed by the easing of a furrowed brow, will tell you immediately that you have just begun the process of letting them downshift from fifth gear to fourth to third . . .

## Asking Without Offending: *Opening the Air Vent*

Even though the Situationally Difficult person is now on the way to fourth or even third gear, asking her the wrong question may send her right back into fifth gear. Some examples of bad (blunt, confrontational, accusatory, sarcastic) questions include:

> *"What the heck is wrong with you?"*
> *"Why are you being so emotional?"*
> *"Why are you taking this out on me?"*
> *"Why do you always act this way?"*
> *"Who spit on your Cheerios this morning?"*

We recommend that you ask questions more effectively by using "probing encouragers." These are questions that encourage more conversation (not just short answers) without any hint of being judgmental. They allow the other side to vent without feeling attacked. Some examples include:

> *"Tell me more."*
> *"Help me understand."*
> *"What happened?"*
> *"Is there anything I can do?"*
> *"Is there anything else?"*

You will note that not all probing encouragers are questions. The first two probing encouragers are probably the most effective because they allow the other side to vent without feeling as if they are being interrogated. Remember, your purpose in asking questions at this point is less about gaining information to solve the problem than it is about taking someone from third down to second and first gear.

### Reassuring Without Solving: *"We'll try" Is a Good Start*

Now that the person is in third, or even second, gear, the human tendency is to start proposing solutions. The problem is, although they have been calmed, they probably are not yet ready to be told what you think that they should do. They need more reassuring before they'll be open to resolution. Examples of attempts at solving rather than reassuring are:

> *"Okay, what you should do is . . ."*
> *"You know what I would do is . . ."*
> *"I think that you need to . . ."*
> *"Make sure you do not . . ."*
> *"Dr. Phil says you should . . ."*
> *"It's pretty obvious that you should . . ."*

Offering your solution as if you have all of the answers the other side lacks may only serve to put them on the defensive and start the escalation process all over again. Instead of telling them what they should so, start by reassuring them that whatever is done, there is a light at the end of the tunnel. Some examples of effective reassuring include:

*"I think that we can get this done."*
*"I hope we can work together on this."*
*"I am willing to do what it takes to move ahead."*
*"I am sure that this can be resolved."*
*"I think we can accomplish our goal."*
*"Based on my experience with others, I think we can get through this."*
*"Let's try to find a way to work this out."*

President Lyndon B. Johnson once said, "Nothing convinces like conviction." By reassuring the Situationally Difficult person, you are demonstrating your conviction that a resolution can be accomplished. Your conviction and demonstration of commitment may convince the other side to downshift from second to first gear, and then into neutral, and begin to work with you to create solutions to what originally seemed to be an insolvable problem. By lending an E.A.R., you've now taken that person from fifth down through the gears all the way to the most productive, nonemotional position, neutral.

All the theories in the world aren't worth a thing unless they're more than theories and work in real life, under the toughest of circumstances, when it looks like nothing is working. Here's a true story, in which Ron lent his E.A.R. to help change fate.

## THE UNLIKELIEST HERO

It was late summer of 1983 and the Orioles were in the thick of the American League pennant race. It was a team full of stars: future Hall of Famers Cal Ripken Jr., Eddie Murray, and Jim Palmer plus a pitching rotation that included Scott McGregor (18–7), Mike Boddiker (16–8), 1983 All-Star Tippy Martinez, and Cy Young winner Mike Flanagan. Orioles manager Joe Altobelli was himself one of the 1983 All-Star coaches. The Orioles of 1983 were a powerhouse baseball team.

But this story is about none of these stars. It's about a lesser-known little guy, a utility infielder named Lenn Sakata. A *hero* named Lenn Sakata. But that comes later.

It was late August and the Orioles and Toronto Blue Jays, coming down the stretch, were in the midst of a pivotal series, perhaps the deciding series as to who went on and who got left behind. To say these games mattered would be a dramatic understatement.

By way of background, during the season, and especially late in the season, one of my clients, that unknown infielder named Lenn Sakata, hadn't been playing much. And he was frustrated. The further the season wore on, the more heated and tighter the race, the less action he seemed to see. For a competitor like Lenn, that just ate away at his guts. He wanted to be on the grass. He wanted to play baseball. Sitting on the bench was tearing him up.

He came to me after the All-Star break, so desperate to play; he said he was ready to be traded. At first, I urged him to just hang in there. Most of all, I counseled him not to vent to the press. With the race gearing up and writers hunting for stories on anything and everything, a discontented player who wanted to be traded was just the kind of meat that would make them salivate. I knew Lenn and, despite his quiet demeanor, I also knew his volatile personality. So far, he'd kept his emotions in check, but he could let go at any time.

Throughout the month of August, his internal turmoil stewed and brewed. Every game he didn't play fed his frustration. Every day on the bench sent him home more pent up.

Finally, on August 24, Lenn Sakata, professional athlete, lifelong competitor, couldn't take it any longer. He picked up the phone and announced, "I've had it." Fortunately, he'd called me instead of calling a sports reporter. In my efforts to get him to regain his calm and not talk to anyone else, I invited him and his wife and, as it turned out, his infant child to my office. When the three arrived, it was clear that Lenn was beyond distraught, doing all he could to keep his anger in check (as I recall, the baby made much less fuss than Lenny). He was at the end of his rope. He wanted to play ball. If that meant being traded, then trade him. I knew I had to say and do whatever I could to try to settle him down. But I also knew there were realities to face. First, agents don't get players traded. Second, general managers like Hank Peters of the Orioles would do whatever they thought best for the team, not one ballplayer. Needless to say, Lenn didn't want to hear those realities. He wanted action that dealt with his reality—not playing baseball.

What could I do? I couldn't do what was beyond my power. I couldn't put him in a ball game. I couldn't make a trade. And I couldn't lie to him. But I could *empathize* with him . . . without agreeing. Empathizing didn't mean I concurred with him that he should demand to be traded. It meant I had personally felt, or could relate to, what he was feeling. Who hasn't been frustrated with playing second (or third) fiddle? Who hasn't had to watch the action from the sidelines? Whether it's in a business transaction, courtroom, a stage, or spat between friends. I told Lenn a story about my early days as a lawyer, sitting next to another attorney who was handling a case I just knew I could've handled better. But it wasn't my call. All I had studied, researched, written, and been trained for was going for naught. The senior lawyer, the general manager of the legal team, had put himself into the game and was losing it. Young Ron Shapiro was just a spectator—a very frustrated, eating-himself-up-inside spectator on the bench or, rather, not allowed to approach the bench. Lenn was barely listening. But "barely" listening was better than not listening at all. Then I told him a couple of baseball stories so much like his, it surprised him. Other ballplayers I'd represented had come to me with virtually the same tale. They too were fierce competitors who were trained to play, not sit on a slab of wood. They'd said, "Play me or trade me." Some were now famous players, having gone on to illustrious careers. Some were just solid, determined, driven athletes who didn't know any other way but to get in the game. He was beginning to hear me. He wasn't alone in this dilemma. He wasn't the only guy to sit on the bench while the game went on. I could see in his eyes, Lenny was listening. His taut, clenched jaw gave just a bit. His grip on the chair loosened. I sensed Lenn had downshifted from fifth to fourth gear.

Next, I began to *ask* Lenn questions. But I didn't bombard him with challenging and/or offending questions like "What good would it do to get traded?" or "Why go sit on another team's bench?" or "Who's going to want a player who hasn't been playing?" Instead, I asked probing encourager-type questions, the kind that would help defuse feelings and further allow Lenn an opportunity to vent. I said, "Lenn, help me understand how a trade might put you in a better position than your current one," and

"Tell me how you would feel if you were traded to a non-contender," and "How would you handle the situation with the Orioles if you were calling the shots?" In the course of hearing nonthreatening questions, mulling them over, and then trying to sincerely answer them, I could visibly note that Lenn was thinking, digesting, and slowly defusing his emotional tension. By my asking questions without offending, he was able to further downshift, from fourth gear to third, from third to second.

Next, I began to *reassure*. I wanted Lenn to leave my office in a better frame of mind than when he entered. But I did not want to overpromise. I didn't want to say, "Lenn, I'll take care of it," when that was well beyond my scope. I didn't want to promise, as we sometimes do with children, "I'll make it all better," when we simply don't have that power. I had to reassure, but without solving. This was all about turning a Situationally Difficult individual into a reasonable, productive individual. I couldn't fix the problem, but I could help lower the temperature of the situation. I reassured by telling him, "I'll work on it for you, but it will take some time." I wasn't fixing, but rather promising to *try*. I slowed his pace by saying, "I understand you feel time has run out, but with another week, I might be able to resolve this and help you take care of things." That kind of reassurance further turned the heat down. A week was, after all, a finite period of time. Anyone could live with a week, especially Lenn, who, when he walked in, seemed like he had a life sentence on the bench. Lenn said, "Yeah, another week would be okay."

That same night I was one of twenty-five-thousand-plus fans at Memorial Stadium for what would be a decisive Orioles versus Blue Jays game. I sat in my usual seat, front row, third base side, just left of the Orioles' dugout. The Orioles were just a game ahead in the standings, and the Blue Jays were looking to make their move. I wasn't surprised but a little disheartened to scan the Orioles' lineup and see that, once again, Lenn Sakata was not penciled in. It looked like he was in for another game with a dugout's-eye view.

The game was a tight one, and inning after inning Orioles manager Joe Altobelli made countless strategic adjustments. Before the top of the eighth, I noticed that Rich Dauer, the second baseman, had not yet emerged from the dugout. Was this it? Knowing that Lenn's skills were best used at second, my hopes went into hypermode and I rose out of my seat to peek into the dugout. Altobelli, pencil in hand, scratched Dauer's name from the lineup card and . . . what was he writing? S–A–K–A . . . *Yes!* My heart pounded. I panned the dugout for Lenny, and there he was, sprinting up the dugout steps, hat pulled down, glove in hand. Finally, after I spent seven frustrating innings watching Lenn's patience grow thinner and thinner, Altobelli provided me (and Lenn) with a huge sigh of relief and sent him in at second base.

When the tenth inning rolled around, after Lenny had scored the tying run in the ninth, I was eagerly anticipating his jog back out to second base. The way I figured it, Altobelli had made so many lineup changes, put in so many pinch hitters in an effort to pull ahead, there was practically no one left, including those in the dugout, who could play the infield other than Lenn. You can imagine my surprise when several guys poured out of the dugout and ran to their positions, but with no sign of Lenn. Still, no one had gone out to second and Lenny was a natural second baseman, so I was confident Lenn was just taking his time and absorbing the moment. But much to my surprise and dismay, Altobelli put another player (an outfielder!), John Lowenstein, in at second instead of leaving Lenny there. Not good! But third base was still vacant, and though Lenn didn't have a typical third baseman's arm, he could play the position well. I was certain Lenn would be moved to third, that is, until total heartbreak set in as Gary Roenicke (a *backup* outfielder!) trotted to third. You can't even fathom my frustration and disappointment in seeing out-of-position players replacing Lenn.

Lenn Sakata was a utility infielder. If there ever was a definition of when and where to use a utility player, this was it. But it appeared that his manager's plan was to put him back on the bench. I could almost feel the churn in Lenn's gut. I was afraid to peer down into the dugout and catch his eye for fear of witnessing a bat-throwing tirade for being overlooked once more.

The only other open position on the field was catcher, but no way would Altobelli put him there. Lenn didn't have a catcher's arm necessary for a pickoff on a steal or to stop a rally. If he wasn't going in at second or third, certainly he wouldn't be behind the plate. But the next thing I saw was five-foot-nine-inch Lenn Sakata, trudging out to the plate, practically swimming in six-foot-one-inch starting catcher Rick Dempsey's oversized chest protector (long enough to protect his knees, ankles, and feet) and shin guards (almost up to his hips). They often call catcher's gear the tools of ignorance, but this was almost ridiculous. I cringed, feeling for Lenn. "He'll be embarrassed at catcher." Still, he was back in the game. Still, I cringed.

In the top of the tenth, the first Blue Jays batter, Cliff Johnson, saved Lenn any shame. The pitch he picked never made it near the catcher's glove. He just crushed the ball, sending it over the outfield wall to give Toronto a 4–3 advantage. With no base runners, Lenn's responsibilities were minimal.

That wasn't to last very long. The next batter, Barry Bonnell, singled, so with a man on base, Lenn's arm was immediately challenged. Bonnell leaned toward second, telegraphing his lack of re-spect, just to "see what Lenn had." What Bonnell didn't see was Orioles first baseman and future Hall of Famer Eddie Murray's signal to the pitcher, Tippy Martinez, for a pickoff play. Tippy Martinez, who had been summoned from the bullpen to face his very first batter, spun and fired to Eddie as Bonnell broke toward second. Eddie promptly tossed the ball to second base, where Bon-nell was tagged out! Lenn's nerves (and his wife's and mine) were spared again. Lenn had still not touched the ball.

The respite was short-lived. Three pitches were thrown to the next batter, Dave Collins, all balls. Then a fourth, another ball, and Collins took first base. Again, the base runner was leaning toward second, ready to test the Orioles, and Lenn in particular. But this time, it was Martinez who had called the pickoff play. As soon as the runner broke from first, he hurled the ball to second and caught Collins in a rundown. Collins was tagged out and there were two outs. Another collective sigh of relief—mine, Lenn's, and his wife's—as Lenn, with a temporary reprieve, watched from home plate.

As if we needed further drama, the Orioles let the Jays extend the inning by allowing a single to the next batter, Willie Upshaw. I have to pause here and say that I've been to a lot of baseball games in my life (it goes with being an agent, a fan, and a father of young ballplayers), but I had never seen, read about, or heard of an entire half-inning expiring from three pickoff plays. That wasn't going to happen. And that meant, short of this rare if not unique circum-stance, Lenn Sakata would have to see defensive action in order to end the inning. Luckily, Eddie Murray and Tippy Martinez weren't worried about what feat had or hadn't ever happened before. Mur-ray again signaled for the pickoff move. Tippy began his windup and the runner broke for second, trying to cover the remaining eighty-five feet to second base. But the windup was a decoy. Instead, Tippy fired to Eddie, who then fired to second, trapping the runner in yet another rundown. They nailed him! We had all just witnessed a great baseball moment, three pickoffs for all three outs in the inning—and Lenny didn't have to make a throw!

Another collective sigh of relief. The undersized catcher in the oversized gear had gotten through the inning unscathed. But then reality returned. The Orioles were still a run down and had only three outs to tie, and then maybe, just maybe, pull this one out.

In the bottom of the tenth, future Hall of Famer and Iron Man Cal Ripken celebrated his birthday by belting a towering solo home run, tying the game 4–4 in typical Cal Ripken clutch form. The Orioles managed to get two men on base, but not before also giving up two outs. The game, the Orioles–Blue Jays series, and perhaps the season, were on the line. All the fans wanted was a miracle. It was a Cal or Eddie moment. But they'd already had theirs, and then some. Instead, little Lenny Sakata, who hadn't played for days and then had come in as the unlikeliest catcher, picked up a bat and walked out to the plate—hardly the image of probable hero. Everyone in Memorial Stadium knew that if Joe Altobelli had any other pinch hitter available, he'd probably have used him.

Lenn managed to take the pitcher, Randy Moffitt, deep into the count. Strikes. Balls. Foul balls. Out of play. Then Lenn saw what he detected to be "his pitch." He swung and the crowd seemed to take one giant breath and hold it. Instead of the famous "crack!" of a Cal Ripken blast, the fans heard a loud "pop!" and saw the ball sail gently, loftily toward the left-field wall. On most days, a hit like that would've drifted lazily down to a waiting outfielder, backpedaling, but not even against the wall. But this ball had just a little more on it, and maybe a little wind behind it . . .

I remember thinking to myself, "No, it's not going to make it. It's short. It's going to drop in play. It's going to be caught." But the ball kept sailing, and maybe Lenn willed it the last few feet, and it dropped on the good side of the wall, the game-winning, Lenn Sakata hero-of-the-day-and-the-series-and-a-chance-at-postseason-play side of the wall. Lenn won the game in extra innings on a three-run home run, only his third home run of the season. The crowd went crazy. His teammates went crazy. And even I got caught up and jumped over the fence protecting my seats, onto the field, got an "okay" nod from the manager and a security guard, and ran to the plate to join the celebration. I hugged Lenn and shouted in his ear, "See, Lenn, I told you we'd work it out!" Lenn Sakata smiled, big and broad and most of all relieved. All the bench-riding tension, all the play-me-or-trade-me ultimatums, all the eating up inside, just disappeared.

We—Lenn and I—had been dealing with a difficult situation. He wasn't being Strategically or Simply Difficult. He had become Situationally Difficult owing to circumstances. His emotions had been ratcheted up, notch after notch, because of an increasingly unpleasant situation. I knew it was within Lenn's character to make the change and to regain his composure and, along with it, his focus and abilities. Inside, he didn't really want to be traded. He wanted, and needed, the opportunity to play. He didn't want to fight with his manager. He wanted to be part of a team fighting for a championship.

Identifying Lenny as being Situationally Difficult, I was able to empathize with him, ask him questions, and reassure him that I would do my best to make things better. I was able to help him downshift from fifth gear to first gear. I believe an angry, irrational, fifth-gear Lenn Sakata would not have connected with that pitch but might have struck out in an explosion of unfocused, frustrated brute power. Instead, a calm, emotionally controlled Lenn Sakata had only one goal on which to concentrate his energies— sending the little white ball 385 feet in the opposite direction.

With a combination of my use of E.A.R., Lenn's baseball prowess, and a little dose of luck, we turned a Situationally Difficult challenge into the opportunity for Lenn to be a hero. He and the Orioles got their World Series rings. No other team he might have been traded to that year could say the same.

## LISTENING WITH YOUR E.A.R.S—THE THREE CS

The entire E.A.R. process has been set up so that people listen rather than respond, preach, solve, talk, deny, denigrate, or dismiss. Again, robotically using E.A.R. may be effective, but using your listening skills to complement this process is typically required to get someone to downshift to neutral.

Unfortunately, there are many courses that teach people how to talk—whether it is a course on diction, a debate class, or a public-speaking program. Unfortunately few, if any, courses teach students how to be more effective listeners. While the old school curriculum focused on the three Rs—reading, 'riting, and 'rithmatic—we teach listening by using the three Cs—connect, consider, and confirm.

### Connect

Connecting includes eye contact, eliminating distractions, not interrupting, and using good body language, but rather than just reminding you of *what to do,* it is a reminder to *do something, any-*

*thing*, to connect. For example, eye contact is hard to establish over the phone, but connecting shouldn't be. Use the person's name and reference subjects of interest to him or her, find and mention mutual acquaintances, and then use the person's name again. When you're in person, besides looking others in the eye, try standing up, taking notes, repeating key points of agreement, whatever works for you. Most important, reduce your distractions. Whether in person or on the phone, stop doing other things: surfing the Web, downloading e-mails, shuffling papers, playing video games, balancing your checkbook, reviewing documents, or trying to quietly eat your lunch. Pay attention to the other person, whether you're across the table or on a tran-atlantic call. Just remember to connect *in some way.*

## Consider

Too often, people are so passionate about their own beliefs, we even fail to consider what the other side is saying. We sometimes even fail to consider what we should say as well. Good listening requires that you slow yourself down; open your mind to opposing views; and then, rather than blurting the first thing that comes to mind, contemplate, deliberate, and reflect before you speak. Knee-jerk reacting is the opposite of listening. Truly consider your response. Do not interrupt. Remember there is a big difference between waiting to speak and actually listening. Pause when the other side finishes speaking so that you consciously gather your thoughts. Acknowledge what they've said. Refrain from making a snap judgment. Even if you're sure of what direction you'd like to go, seek more information. Careful consideration not only allows you to formulate a response, but it also sends a message that what the other side had to say merits your careful reflection.

## Confirm

Confirmation is critical and needs to be done before, during, and after a meeting or conversation. Confirm beforehand by setting an agenda, in writing, or clearly stating objectives at the beginning of an exchange. Confirmation during the conversation includes re-stating of key issues and making clarifying remarks. After the conversation takes place, it is important to confirm what was said by summarizing all the critical points. Summation may be a verbal report at the end or, in more formal situations, an e-mail or written digest or recap is appropriate. No matter the situation, confirmation is critical. It prevents errors and misunderstandings.

The key to listening is that anyone can and should do it. There's no secret formula on how to be a great listener. We all have the ability; it's just a matter of being cognizant of our behavior and adapting it as needed, and then consciously applying it. The three Cs give you a simple, comprehensive system to improve your listening skills.

---

# CHAPTER TWELVE

# Little Big Man
## *Controlling the Encounter with the Strategically Difficult*

## DIFFICULT BEHAVIOR AS A PROVEN STRATEGY

A S WE POINTED OUT earlier, Strategically Difficult people can make you feel as if they're "up to something." They try to convince you (by persuasion or by mandate) that you must play by their rules. They use difficult behavior as a tool, one that has proven to be effective in the past, one that they may have honed until it is the most powerful weapon in their business or personal interaction arsenal. It is truly a strategy, complete with tested tactics. They have a prescribed set of rules. Most important, they will attempt to pressure, maneuver, or railroad you into playing by their rules. However, since they are strategic—not just responding to a bad situation or acting difficult for its own sake—they can be made to alter or modify behavior, and even retreat from a position, if dealt with deftly and wisely, with effective counterstrategy. The following is a simple, clear methodology for dealing with tactics: the three Rs.

## THE THREE RS: RECOGNIZE, RESPOND, AND REDIRECT

This system consists of another set of threes (easy to remember, easy to apply).

### Recognize: *Trusting Your "Sixth Sense"*

Before you can defend against a Strategically Difficult person's tactic, you must recognize the possibility that a tactic is being used. The fastest way to learn to recognize tactics is by familiarizing yourself with the Top Twenty Tactics (page 96). Familiarity will help train your brain to recognize the most common tactics the moment they are employed against you. But, as is often the case in business and life in general, your gut—or built-in radar—may be as reliable as your brain. As part of recognizing the tactics of a Strategically Difficult person, we advise you to use your "sixth sense." Some people call this gut guide by names such as instinct or intuition, but regardless of its name, your sixth sense is actually your subconscious telling you something is wrong long before your conscious mind can understand and process what is happening. Many dog and cat owners will attest to their animal's sixth sense. And many human beings swear they have experiences with this inexplicable sense.

Mark has a black Labrador retriever named Lou who is one of the happiest dogs in the world and greets everyone with his tail wagging. But if Mark's wife, Lori, comes home upset, Lou can pick up on it almost instantly and greets her with head bowed and bent ears. Lou has no idea exactly what is wrong, but he senses that something is upsetting Lori (Mark has mentioned that he sometimes wishes his own sixth sense toward Lori were equally well refined).

Humans often express their own feelings of possessing this sixth sense. Alice Rose, an associate who works in our office, tells us she once woke up and found herself standing at the edge of her bed with a blanket she had taken from the closet during her first and only sleepwalking event. She had dreamt her mother, who lives in Chicago, was cold and needed a blanket. Before Alice Rose could call and tell her mom about her experience, her mom called to say, "I think I caught a cold. I kicked off my blankets last night and I nearly froze!"

Maybe it was just a coincidence. Or maybe not.

Learn to trust what you feel. Whether you call it a sixth sense or instinct or gut feeling, our subconscious mind often knows that danger lies ahead well before our conscious mind can recognize the actual warning signs. The same applies to the tactics used by Strategically Difficult people. We may not know the name of the tactic, its details, or its impact upon us, but we just know, in our gut, something is not right. When we teach, we don't encourage paranoia. But we do encourage you to listen to your inner voice, especially when it whispers, "Watch out."

## NUCLEAR POWER
### *Or How Admiral Rickover Won Small Battles*

Admiral Hyman Rickover, child of a Jewish immigrant family, entered the Naval Academy in 1918, almost immediately in conflict with its traditional W.A.S.P. aristocracy. According to much of the history written about him, Rickover was unpopular with other midshipmen and was resented as a loner. He graduated from the academy and went on to an early career that was largely undistinguished. He volunteered for submarine duty and served, but he was not selected for command. Shortly after, he was selected, almost randomly, for a limited assignment to Oak Ridge, Tennessee, where nuclear research was being performed. He quickly determined that the military use of nuclear power represented a future opportunity for the navy and for Hyman Rickover. From then on, it became his obsession and eventual path to a historic role in U.S. naval history.

However, despite his increasing renown and respect in the field, rising to the rank of admiral, gaining international eminence, Rickover never seemed to lose the insecurity that came with being an outsider in his early years. The father of the "nuclear navy" and developer of the world's first nuclear-powered submarine, the admiral became infamous for his subtle but highly effective interpersonal tactics. The classic Rickover maneuver was to position visitors—be they important government officials or departmental subordinates—in purposely unbalanced chairs. He literally kept those he dealt with off-balance when they were in his office. The admiral was employing Tactic 11—Physical Surroundings—to gain or maintain a sense of superiority and, consequently, an upper hand in dealing with others. Most of the people who sat in his office probably could not identify the physical manipulation—the rocky, uneven chair legs, their own literal instability versus Rickover's solid, steady position—but they would say that they simply felt uncomfortable or at a disadvantage in his presence.

In day-to-day life, you face tactics regularly, almost routinely. When you try to pin a used-car salesman down to a firm, final deal, and he says, "I'll have to go in the back to check with my manager," you may not be able to label his ploy as Tactic 1—Higher Authority—but you probably do have a gut feeling something is not right, or out of your control, at that moment.

Even if you can't name every one, if you make yourself familiar with the Top Twenty Tactics, you should become comfortable relying on your gut as a radar device for detecting tactics. We encourage you to memorize these tactics because knowing all of them will help you identify them. But we also encourage you to learn to tune in to what your subconscious is telling you. To invert an old phrase, "If it doesn't feel good, do not do it." Therefore, whether it is through memorization or intuition, the first step in dealing with a Strategically Difficult person's tactics is to recognize each tactic. Once you have recognized its use, you're prepared to disarm it.

### Respond: *Verbalizing Without Demonizing*

When someone is being strategically nasty, they are typically engaged in a behavior that has worked for him or her in the past, often because the other side was unaware that such a tactic was being used against them. The Strategically Difficult person is relying on future victims being just as naïve or uninitiated as to the nature of his or her ruse.

We therefore recommend that a primary method for controlling Strategically Difficult people is to clearly make them aware that you are "in on their game." By providing an early, simple response that reveals your awareness of their potential use of a tactic, you demonstrate to them that you're no easy mark.

*Caution:* Try *not* to use an accusatory tone when making this response. You do not want to embarrass or threaten Strategically Difficult people, as this might make them dig their heals in further and display even more difficult behavior. We advise you to avoid making statements such as:

> *"I know what you are up to."*
> *"Your tricks will not work against me."*
> *"Stop trying to manipulate me."*
> *"Your tactics are insulting."*

There are two reasons using these types of accusatory statements will likely be ineffective. First, the person you're dealing with may, in fact, not be using a tactic. There is no way that you can be 100 percent sure 100 percent of the time that someone's actions are intentional. Your accusations could be inaccurate. Second, you may be backing that person into a corner. While you want to make the other side aware that you are not being duped by his tactic, you also want to leave him a way to save face by discontinuing the use of the tactic. If you attack him directly, he may go into a defense mode. The conversation could then become bogged down in a "he said/she said" exchange, focused on tactics rather than on an exploration of how to solve the issue at hand.

So, what are some effective ways to articulate what you are experiencing? Getting your observation out and stated will take you a long way toward resolution. Try these approaches.

*Express your feelings.* While someone can deny that they are trying to manipulate you, there is no way that they can tell you that you are not "feeling" manipulated. For example:

- In response to Tactic 11—Physical Surroundings—try "You know, I am not comfortable with these surroundings. Let's say that we move to a setting where we're both more at ease."
- In response to Tactic 3—Take It or Leave It—try "I'm feeling like I am being backed into a corner with a take-it-or-leave-it, no-choices-type approach. I'm not sure that this is the most productive way for us to move forward."
- In response to Tactic 9—Outrageous Behavior—try "I am feeling that emotions are overwhelming our rational exchange and that is not going to lead to a good outcome."

*Cite prior experiences.* By telling someone you have been in similar situations previously, it indicates that you're not a rube. But it does not directly accuse the other side of being the kind of person who would premeditatedly use the type of manipulation you've faced in the past. Consider these possible responses:

- In response to Tactic 13—Surprise Information—try "I have been in other situations where new information came in late in the process, much like it has here. I have to tell you, in my previous experiences, it hurt or even killed the deal."
- In response to Tactic 10—Nibbling—try "I've been told to be careful when the other side starts to make additional requests or demands near the end of a deal. I hope we're not going to start to renegotiate this thing so late in the process."
- In response to Tactic 12—Ganging Up—try "I was expecting this to be a one-on-one meeting. It has always been my experience that the best results come when the teams are even, not stacked against one side or the other."

*Make light of the tactic.* Rather than reacting overtly to the use of the tactic, try to purposely make light of its use. Of course, the key to making light is making the comment in the right tone. If delivered in a "good old boy" type of style, it can be friendly yet disarming. A stronger tone, however, might be accusatory and could put the other side in the defensive mode.

As with all lessons, make sure you interpret and modify them to best fit your own style. If you are not normally an easygoing type and are seen as more intense and aggressive, you simply may not be believable as a good old boy or good old girl. On the other hand, if you do possess a likable, relaxed demeanor, one that makes others feel comfortable, this may be the ideal way for you to disarm a tactic.

To make light of a tactic, we actually advocate naming the specific tactic. We believe that because the appropriate delivery will be charmingly candid, rather than accusatory, the direct approach can be used without putting the other side on the defensive. Some examples:

- In response to Tactic 2—Good Cop/Bad Cop—try "Hmm, feels like good cop/bad cop. I think I've seen this movie before."
- In response to Tactic 7—Silence—try "Okay, whose favorite song is 'The Sounds of Silence'?"
- In response to Tactic 8—The Red Herring—try "Call me a crazy fisherman, but I think somebody just tried to lure me away from the real point with irrelevant bait, a.k.a. a red herring."

What follows is a case in point that highlights two of the three Rs—recognize and respond—and then allows for the third—redirect. It's a real-life business adventure that Ron experienced in his celebrity agent days, involving a Strategically Difficult counterpart who was anything but subtle, and almost comical, in his attempted use of manipulative tactics.

## LITTLE BIG MAN

I recall some dealings I had with the talented but egotistical president of a prominent ad agency. He would insist that every meeting we had take place at his building, in his own corner office. He always seated his visitors opposite his oversized desk, in very low chairs (truly, almost ottoman height) with what must have been custom-shortened legs. I could drop my arm down and rest my palm on the floor. In contrast, the president's own desk was literally up on a pedestal, a full step or two above the floor of the office. His chair (or throne) had an adjustment that ratcheted him up even further, into a lofty position. The result? Not surprising. All guests, suppliers, applicants, and even clients were constantly reminded, in a none-too-subtle way, that they were in the presence of someone who was "bigger," someone with more stature, more power, and, of course, more control.

One day, I again found myself at the ad agency for yet another meeting, this time representing an athlete who was to be the spokesman for an ad campaign. I walked in and was escorted to my designated seat. I lowered (and lowered and lowered) myself down, sat for a minute or two in my little dollhouse chair, grazing my knuckles on the polished floor, tilting my head up at the agency CEO, absorbing my growing discomfort within this environment, and *recognizing* that my sixth sense was telling me something wasn't right. It even reminded me of a story I'd heard about President Lyndon Johnson.

L.B.J. always sat in his own, reserved commander-in-chief "high chair" whenever he flew on Air Force One. Already a large and imposing man, the chair lifted him further above his staff, advisers, underlings, party leaders of both sides, and, not insignificantly, the press. At no time could any guest aboard Air Force One forget that this was the president's airplane, that the president was in charge, and that the president was Lyndon Baines Johnson. Guests were there strictly at the will and whim of President Johnson, the man in the higher chair. Perhaps my host had been impressed with the same story.

Sitting in the ad agency office, I thought and sensed and felt, and even engaged in a bit of small talk (pun intended). But finally, when the conversation began to head toward my client's impending endorsement contract, I stood up (not that it was easy to get out of my chair), saying, "I feel better if I walk when I talk." This allowed me to *respond* by verbalizing my feelings in a way that was neither accusing nor demonizing.

The president's eyes followed me cautiously. I was no longer almost reclining but still a step or two down from the president. We began to discuss the basic parameters of the deal. As we got to the meat of the contract, I climbed up to the pedestal level. The president's eyes widened, but he couldn't really protest. I walked over to speak to him more intimately—after all, we were now at the crux of our agreement. I then leaned over the president's chair (putting him in a position from which he had to look up at me) and asked some probing questions, focusing on the critical deal points. Once I had recognized and responded, I was prepared to *redirect* our focus to the business at hand. (More on the third R to come . . .)

At this juncture, his seeming advantage was neutralized. He didn't have the upper position, upper chair, upper level, or upper hand, in any way. In fact, by trusting my instincts and then verbalizing my feelings, I was in a position to refocus and get to our real business, now with the momentum reversed in my favor.

### Redirect: *Focusing on the Issue at Hand*

This last step for dealing with tactics is vital because it prevents the conversation from getting derailed into a discussion about the tactic rather than the topic that brought you to the table. Once you have made the other side aware that you're aware of their tactic, immediately refocus the conversation back to the issues at hand. If you force the other side to defend themselves, then you are going to have to justify each of your statements, consider their rationale, rebut, and so on, until you are way off track, far from the business at hand. Prevent this diversion by using statements such as:

> *"Regardless of how I feel, the most important thing is that we get this resolved."*
>
> *"I am sure that my experiences in the past are not repeating themselves here, so let's just move on."*
>
> *"Of course, I know the most important thing to both of us is to get this all done as quickly as possible."*
>
> *"We have done such a good job of moving this issue forward, let's keep it on track and not get distracted by these other little things."*
>
> *"We agreed earlier on the three things we wanted to get out of this conversation, and I want to make sure we stay focused on those three things."*

The exact words of such refocusing statements are less important than the concept of not getting "stuck" in the analysis, discussion, defense, rebuttal, and ensuing derailment as a result of the tactic that was or was not used. Keep it simple: recognize, respond, and redirect.

*Note:* Do not be fooled. Simple does not mean easy. These tools may be simple to learn, but they require implementation and practice to master. The more you use them, the more effective they will be.

What follows is one of the more vivid and indelible illustrations of the masterful use of the Three Rs, which occurs in Tom

Wolfe's novel *A Man in Full*. Wolfe's two protagonists, both consummate power brokers and deal makers, spar for dominance. In the end, however, it is the one who is most deft at being able to recognize, respond, and redirect who renders the other almost impotent.

## THE SADDLEBAGS SCENE FROM *A MAN IN FULL*

Wolfe sets the scene by pitting two accomplished negotiators in a macho showdown. Charlie Croker is a megadeveloper, described as "almost bald, but his baldness was the kind that proclaims *masculinity to burn*—as if there was so much testosterone surging up through his hide it had popped the hair right off of his head." At the time of this scene in the book, Croker owes the bank over five hundred million dollars, and the bank has assigned their big gun, Harry Zale, to make sure the debt is collected. Wolfe depicts Zale as a "drill instructor," explaining that "Harry liked to refer to what was about to take place not as a workout session but as boot camp."

Harry Zale starts the battle by carefully, almost diabolically, creating an extremely uncomfortable, inescapable environment for Croker (Tactic 11—Physical Surroundings). Zale's goal was to put Croker under such pressure that the sweat pouring from his body would produce "saddlebags" on his shirt. Croker is guided to a stiff chair that faces the window in such a way that the sun sears into his eyes. Almost prophetically, there is a dead plant across the room from Croker. Furthermore, Zale has surrounded this wealthy, self-absorbed, discriminating mogul with furniture that is cheap, frayed, and worn. Even the carpet is threadbare. In case Croker thinks he will be treated with deference, the shoddy surroundings quickly make clear the opposite. From the outset, though, Croker and his people can't put their finger on the exact negative signals, they *recognize* something, some things, is very, very wrong. As Wolfe writes, "At first they merely sensed them, stimulus by stimulus, through their antennae, through the hair on their arms. It was the central nervous system that finally informed the tycoon."

No innocent to sophisticated negotiation ploys, Croker *responds* to the situation by launching into a diatribe about how he, the bank's supposed prized customer, had been made many promises in the past, promises that were not fulfilled.

But Harry Zale just as quickly *recognizes* Croker's tactic. The distraction (Tactic 8—The Red Herring) of the bank's broken promises was intended to shift Harry onto other subjects. The accompanying focus on other issues (Tactic 15—Smoke Screen) was meant to force such confusion that the meeting would finally disintegrate without resolution. Letting Croker know, in unmistakable terms, that he is not going to be taken in by these two tactics of confusion, Zale himself bluntly *responds,* "I'd like to hear some simple proposals as to how we are gonna get paid back. Simple, no assembly necessary, batteries included."

Up to this point, the match has been pretty even, with the two all-star deal makers facing off across the table, neither one blinking. Despite Zale's putting Croker in a hothouse, Croker doesn't wilt. He counters with his own moves. And despite Zale's consistently spotting and blunting Croker's methods, Croker isn't about to throw in the towel. Croker continues trying to employ more distractions (Tactic 15—Smoke Screen), then new facts (Tactic 13—Surprise Information), and even unconventional actions (Tactic 8—Outrageous Behavior) to keep Harry from getting through to him.

But once again, Harry is smart enough to continuously *redirect* Croker to the issue at hand through "a round of verbal fencing in which [Harry] kept cutting off Croker's evasions, blusters, rambles, tangents, until finally, Croker was in a corner where there was nothing to do but come out with the damning information."

Exasperated, Croker claims that there are just no assets to sell that can make up the five hundred million dollars the bank is owed. It's a blatant lie, but Harry is prepared. Instead of swallowing Croker's claim of poverty, instead of debating *whether* Croker's assets are gone, Zale *redirects* the conversation to *how to* repay the debt. Harry, anticipating all of Croker's moves, has come armed with a list of properties and goods held by Croker. Zale spells out what Croker should and will do with these assets:

"The company cars worth $593,000 . . . Sell 'em."

"The fleet of airplanes estimated at $58 million . . . Sell 'em."

"The farm, game preserve, and stud farm . . . Sell 'em."

Croker, trapped in a sleazy room full of run-down furnishings, staring into the sun, the thermostat rising, faced with undeniable facts, beaten at his own game of guts negotiating, was simply all out of ploys and tricks. He used his best tactics, but Zale countered each and every one with the three Rs. Croker is limp, a man laden with saddlebags of sweat and defeat. In the end, Harry won the battle because of his ability to recognize the tactics being used against him, to respond when he felt he was being manipulated, and to redirect the conversation with a laser focus.

## COUNTER EVERY TACTIC

Remember the Top Twenty Tactics? Next we offer an invaluable tool with which to identify, disarm, or avoid altogether—utilizing the three Rs—these tactics. We call it the Tactic Deactivator. You can simply use it as a reference guide when needed. Since virtually every tactic you encounter is one of these or a variation on one of them, just refer back to the guide, spot your tactic, and follow the steps to counter it.

## THE TACTIC DEACTIVATOR: COUNTERTACTICS FOR THE TOP TWENTY TACTICS

### 1. Higher Authority
Once a final decision is agreed upon (or seems to be agreed upon), the other side claims he or she lacks the power to make the decision really final or official.

### Countertactics
- *Smoke out the tactic early.* Ask "What is your decision-making process?" Determine whether there's anyone else whom they might use as a higher authority.
- *Ask for a meeting with the higher authority.* Defuse the mysterious power of the higher authority.
- *Match their higher authority to yours.* You too must go to someone to get the agreement approved.
- *Draw upon their ego.* Ask "If you approve this deal, is your boss likely to back you?"
- *Ask for a positive recommendation.* Receive at least a small commitment from the person with whom you are conversing.
- *Put the "deal" in writing.* Avoid the situation where your counterpart claims to have "misunderstood" you.

### 2. Good Cop/Bad Cop

Two people are involved on the other side in a deal or negotiation. One acts like your advocate or ally while the other acts like your adversary, manipulating you the entire time.

#### Countertactics

- *Call their game.* Say "This feels a lot like good cop/ bad cop."
- *Ignore the bad cop.* Let the bad cop expel his energy so you can move forward and focus on the business at hand.
- *Terminate the session.* Turn to the good cop and tell him that it's obvious the other person—the bad cop—is too upset to carry on.

### 3. Take It or Leave It

This is the no-negotiation posture of "My first offer is my final offer."

#### Countertactics

- *Expand the possibilities.* Ask "What if we were able to come up with a deal that is even better for you than the one on the table?"
- *Break it down.* Ask "What part of the offer is final? Price? Quantity? Deadline?"
- *Take it . . . conditionally.* Tell the other side you will take the deal provided you're able to get agreement on other items that are important to you.
- *Ignore it.* Sometimes ignoring the threat of a final offer eliminates its impact.

### 4. False Deadlines

The other side creates an arbitrary time pressure (that seems real) in order to try and make you come to an agreement that may not be ideal.

#### Countertactics

• *Question the cause.* Ask "What's creating the time pressure? Is there anything that you can do to help relieve the deadline pressure?"
• *Determine what happens after the deadline.* Ask "What if we don't make it?"
• *Suggest a trade.* Ask "What if I could take a little more time, but come back to the table with a substantially better deal?"

### 5. Passive-Aggressive

In the midst of "dealing," the other person will stop dealing and shut down. It is a seeming sabotage of the deal with inaction, again aimed at getting you to accept optimal terms.

#### Countertactics

• *Put it back on their plate.* Ask "What do you think? What would you do in my shoes?" Questions force the ball into their court and keep you from revealing too much.
• *Use silence to your advantage.* Avoid filling the void by talking and possibly giving in. Say "Take your time. I'm under no pressure to get this resolved this minute."
• *Apply deadline pressure.* They draw out dialogue so you feel time pressure to make concessions and make progress.

Instead, set firm deadlines and hold their feet to the fire when the deadlines arrive.

• *Ask them what it will take.* Rather than trying to figure out how to make them happy, get them to commit by asking them, "What will it take to get you to agree?"

## 6. The Wince

You make an offer and the other person reacts with an exaggerated facial expression to get you to question the reasonableness of your offer. His face seems to say, "Oh my God, you must be kidding!" or "You're out of your mind!"

### Countertactics

• *Repeat the offer.* The other person is expecting you to react. If you keep your calm, they'll see their gambit isn't working and will likely give it up.

• *Ask them what they were expecting.* If they offer anything, you now have the bargaining range. If they make a ridiculous offer, at least you have not bid against yourself.

• *Walk.* Tell them it's obvious that because the two sides are so far apart, there's no reason to continue. If they let you walk, it was true. If they stop you, your offer was worth continuing the discussion.

## 7. Silence

The other person simply creates ominous "dead space" that may intimidate you into disclosing important information or even capitulating on a key point.

**Countertactics**

• *Match silence with silence.* There is no obligation for you to respond instantly, so take your time when the other side is taking their time.

• *Ask a question.* Some people think when there is silence that the first to speak loses. Not so, especially if you ask a question such as "Do you need more time to think about this?"

• *Engage another.* If the other side has two team members and one goes silent, ask the other person what they think, forcing a response from one or the other team members.

## 8. The Red Herring

The other side focuses on unimportant details (acting as if they are important) in order to divert attention from the real deal points.

**Countertactics**

• *Ask for explanations.* Forcing the other side to make it clear why this new issue is essential may demonstrate its actual lack of importance.

• *Table it.* Discuss the more important issues without being distracted by the red herring. After a deal is worked out, the other side will be less likely to lose ground by refocusing on the red herring.

• *Force prioritization.* Ask what concessions the other side is prepared to make if you'll concede the red herring issue. Typically, the other side won't be willing to concede on issues valued more than the red herring.

### 9. Outrageous Behavior

The person on the other side is given to sudden, loud outbursts or other socially errant behavior—again, to take the focus off of the real issues.

### Countertactics

• *Be prepared.* Research should determine if this type of behavior is expected and will enable you to keep calm when the outburst occurs.

• *Remember, if it's business, it's only business.* Outrageous behavior should not be taken personally and doesn't warrant concessions.

• *Send in a proxy.* If you can't face the other person calmly, send in someone who can.

### 10. Nibbling

The deal seems to be set. Then the other side makes a small (so it seems) addition at the eleventh hour. Then another small addition. And another.

### Countertactics

• *Nibble back.* By demonstrating your willingness to trade nibbles, it will make the other side less likely to continue the tactic.

• *Write it down.* Keep documentation of discussions. Then point out that the issue wasn't discussed but that you're willing to open it if the other side will also discuss additional items you'd like to raise.

• *Ask if it is a deal breaker.* Force the other side to admit that it is not that important to them.

## 11. Physical Surroundings

The other side controls a venue to gain an advantage, such as controlling your comfort level, location, resources, and so on.

### Countertactics

- *Change locations.* Insist on a meeting location conducive to good discussion.
- *Change positions.* Simply don't sit in the low chair or the one that faces the glare.
- *Change the time.* Additional time you buy by rescheduling allows you to be better prepared.

## 12. Ganging Up

You are dealing one-on-one with another person. Without warning, he or she brings someone else to the bargaining table. You are outnumbered and possibly outflanked by expertise or rank.

### Countertactics

- *Find the "weakest link."* If one person on the other side is empathetic to your cause, or at least not as opposed, focus time and attention on that person.
- *Get commitments without giving commitments.* If the other side has assembled all decision makers in an attempt to intimidate, ask that a decision be made immediately, as they do not have to check with anyone.
- *Ignore the rest of their team.* Bring the conversation back to one key person so that the other side cannot bombard you from all sides.

### 13. Surprise Information

After exploring a potential deal and supposedly putting all relevant data on the table, the other side introduces new information, catching you off guard and unprepared.

### Countertactics

- *Take a time-out.* Slow the process down. If information is new, demand time to process it before you make commitments. Ask what would happen if a decision were not made immediately. If you must give an answer now, the answer is no, but it might be yes if you're given time to think about it.

- *Reopen all issues.* By reopening all items when surprise information is introduced, you may be able to better your previously agreed-to position.

### 14. Trust Me

The other person tries to force concessions from you with fantasy promises of making it up to you in some future but indeterminate deal.

### Countertactics

- *Back-end triggers.* Instead of accepting a later promise from them, reposition their request so you get what you want *first,* at which point it will *then* "trigger" the concession they requested.

- *Ask for a current favor.* Ask "What other deals could you show me that we could get agreement on immediately?"

- *Ask for more than verbal assurances.* Ask "To make sure the next person understands the agreement, let's put it in writing, an e-mail, or an amendment to the contract?"

### 15. Smoke Screen

Employing a strategy of planned obfuscation, the other side deliberately confuses the issues, facts, and figures so that you lose track of key elements or, by the time you return to them, are less intent on their exact definitions.

#### Countertactics

- *Clarify.* After they give a long-winded response, summarize key information you wanted to obtain.
- *Ask the same question again.* After you wait patiently through one of their rambling responses, say, "I appreciate that and what I'd like to understand is . . ."
- *Ask them to summarize.* Review all information provided to make sure that the summary is correct and that there are no hidden time bombs.

### 16. Denial

The other side simply denies having agreed to a point that had clearly been agreed upon earlier, in order to reopen it and win the point back.

#### Countertactics

- *Identify the misunderstanding.* By identifying the misunderstanding without accusing someone of lying, you defuse the tactic unemotionally.
- *Reopen issues.* If previously agreed-to items are now taken off the table, you need to reopen other issues that you agreed to.
- *Get it in writing.* Create a paper trail and prevent future denial of points previously agreed to.

### 17. The Bluff

The other side tells you something that may or may not be true, yet you are suspicious.

*Countertactics*

- *Ask for documentation.* Tell the other side that you need to see the bid to make sure that they are providing the same terms and conditions that you are, or blame a higher authority. Say "I need to take the competing bid back to my partners so that they know the entire situation."
- *Ask for clarification.* This might make the other side feel nervous about continuing their bluff for fear they have scared you away.
- *Call the bluff.* Sometimes the only way to test the bluff is to walk away, but be careful to leave the door open, saying, "We cannot under those conditions, but if things don't work out as you wish, feel free to come back."

### 18. Controlling the Contract

The other side drafts the contract after agreement and, to your detriment, makes changes to which you had not agreed, usually to gain an advantage after you think the deal is done.

*Countertactics*

- *Write drafts of the contract.* That way the other side is reacting to your draft rather than you reacting to theirs.
- *Write a memo before you write a contract.* You'll get both parties to agree to the main agreements before lawyers start to confuse the issues with "legalese."
- *Manage the lawyers.* Make sure to reestablish contact with

the other side to reiterate your understandings before you
let the lawyers battle it out.

• *Personalize communication.* Before you get into a battle of
contracts, pick up a phone and speak to the person with
whom you made the deal.

## 19. Withdrawal

The other side, suddenly and precipitously, retracts a proposal so
as to force hurried acceptance.

### Countertactics

• *Use a hypothetical.* Ask "*If* you were able to get it past
your board, would you be willing to continue the
conversation?" If the other side agrees, then you've
prevented the withdrawal.

• *Offer mutual concessions.* This gives the other parties a
potential reason to return but does not provide them with a
unilateral gain.

• *Focus on previous progress.* Even if there is frustration at
this point, past progress should justify that the other side
will not just walk away.

## 20. Monetary Concessions

These are sneaky pleas or suggestions by your adversary to get you
to reveal your price and/or lower your price, so that he can hold
you to that number and convince you that you made an offer.

### Countertactics

• *Buy more time.* If the other side says, "Give me a ballpark
price," say that you'd rather think about the issue in order
to make a more realistic assessment. If this isn't possible,

lowball your ballpark price to prevent getting locked into a bad deal.

- *Call their bluff.* If the other side demands, "You have to do better than that," replying "How much better do I have to do?" forces your opponent to commit to a number *before* you bid against yourself.
- *Split the difference.* Try to set the split-the-difference price as a bottom and continue to discuss from there.

# CHAPTER THIRTEEN

# Free Agents Always Go for the Money

*Controlling the Encounter with the Simply Difficult*

## THE DIFFERENCE BETWEEN *ACTING* DIFFICULT AND *BEING* DIFFICULT

For the Simply Difficult person, using power isn't a strategy; it's an imperative. It is part and parcel of this person's being. This is distinctly different from the Situationally Difficult or Strategically Difficult types, both of whom *act* difficult but may not in fact *be* difficult.

The Simply Difficult person is not reactively responding to a situation—environment, circumstances, pressures, outside forces, bad news, stresses, moods, or emotional swings. Nor is the Simply Difficult person proactively following a strategy—skillfully, surgically, judiciously, efficiently, for maximum effect. On the contrary, the Simply Difficult person is just that, simply, plainly, innately, intrinsically difficult.

He or she wields raw power. The Simply Difficult person is often called "power mad," manifesting his or her behavior in wild irrationality, arbitrary rules, punishments, or consequences randomly enacted, without regard for outcomes, simply because the power exists. "I have power; therefore I use it." Each use is a reaffirmation that this person is in charge. You are face-to-face with the ultimate table-pounding, chair-throwing, poking, jabbing, storming in, storming out, screaming, yelling, threatening dictator-despot-bully-tyrant-impossible-person!

In dealing with Simply Difficult people, you must become as well versed in raw power as they are. Unlike the Simply Difficult person, however, you do not have to abuse power in order to use it.

## YOU HAVE MORE POWER THAN YOU THINK

Before talking about how to deal with Simply Difficult people, it is important to point out that most people have infinitely more power than they believe they have. But people fail to recognize how much power, and as a result, they give in too easily. In reality, they could have better handled the Simply Difficult people by learning how to look deeply at their situation and discern the power they do have. Eleanor Roosevelt once said, "No one can take advantage of you without your permission." While it may seem a cliché to say, "The power is within you," there is truth to it. The key is finding and then amplifying it.

## THE A.B.C.S OF DEALING WITH A SIMPLY DIFFICULT PERSON

Typically the use of power by a Simply Difficult person is unbridled, uncontrolled, crude, very raw. The power is unleashed to create an environment that spins out of control. Conversely, in order to regain control of the encounter, you must understand the source of the other person's power, find a way to build your own power to match his or her power, and make sure to effectively communicate your message to the other side. To accomplish these goals, we have created a three-step method that we call the A.B.C.s:

**A**scertain sources of power: *Before you can control the encounter,*
*you must understand the source of a Simply Difficult person's*
*power. Comprehending from where the Simply Difficult*
*person's source of power emanates is critical to helping you*
*create a strategy to negate that power.*

**B**alance the power: *Just as every power has a source, there also*
*exists a counterbalance to that power. By finding and*
*identifying the counterbalance(s), rather than fighting an*
*uphill battle, you can employ ways to level the playing field.*

**C**ommunicate consequences: *As in most life encounters, style*
*and effectiveness of communication are as important as the*
*facts communicated. Sheer confrontations of power versus*
*power will almost always escalate. To prevent the escalation,*
*you must successfully put across to the other side not only that*
*you possess power but also what the ultimate outcome or*
*consequences could or would be if you use yours against theirs.*

Make no mistake—controlling the encounter with Simply Difficult people is a daunting challenge. But mastering the process that can manage such an encounter can be achieved with a little practice and, in the end, can change the outcome of what seemed like an impossible altercation.

## Ascertain Source of Power

The first step in controlling the encounter with a Simply Difficult person is to determine his or her exact source of power. Too often we are instantly intimidated by the fact that the Simply Difficult person possesses power, and we reflexively fall into a fight-or-flight mode. To avoid this mistake, when facing a person you suspect of being Simply Difficult, get in the habit of engaging the rational mind before falling prey to any reaction. Using your rationality, ask yourself to really think about, analyze, and determine this person's source of power. Just by posing that question in your own mind—by entering into a mental exploration (rather than an emotional knee-jerk response)—you will neutralize your emotions. What you have now done is begun a process that will help you overcome that use of power by the Simply Difficult person. You must first understand the power before you can fight the power.

Some experts at analyzing the roots of power have utilized labels such as: "The Forty-eight Laws of Power," or "The Twelve Types of Ultimate Power," and many other similarly comprehensive examinations, all of which are possibly helpful. However, we believe most challenges in life are less complicated than they appear, and, consequently, most good systems for dealing with challenges can also be simplified. We believe virtually all power derives not from forty-eight or twelve or one hundred rules, secrets, or supplies, but from three basic sources: Authoritative power, Punishment power, and Resource power.

Typically, a Simply Difficult person will possess more than one, and usually at least two, of these sources of power. For example, you may occupy a position of authority, but it may not give you power if you have no resources with which to back your authority. You may have resources that could give you power, but lacking punishment power, those resources may never be utilized and, therefore, may mean little. It is important to look at the combination of the three sources listed above both separately and in combination.

*Authoritative Power* It's generally accepted that people in positions of authority possess power. We expect the boss to have power over employees, the policeman to have power over citizens, the doctor to have power over patients, and the pastor to have power over the congregation. In most daily situations, society's granting these people power makes perfect sense. Bestowing authoritative power to others is a necessity—an efficiency—in a complex society. When a police officer turns on the flashing lights and siren, drivers should pull their cars over. When a physician prescribes a certain treatment, patients trust the medical expertise. When a religious leader tells congregants that they should pray for others, most do so faithfully. When a boss asks an employee to stay late to finish an important project, a typical worker accepts it without question.

Problems arise, however, when a Simply Difficult person abuses his authoritative power. Consider these examples: the police officer who takes the law into his own hands, as we have seen in brutal videotaped beatings, the doctor who stands to gain personally from promoting certain types of unproven treatments, the religious figure who becomes cultlike and leads his people to mass suicide, the boss who uses the threat of power to sexually harass.

Authoritative power isn't restricted to the obvious practitioners, such as political and military leaders—from Rasputin to Hitler to Idi Amin to Saddam Hussein. Authoritative power resides wherever an individual has the official and accepted sanction of bestowed power. The challenge most people face is being able to look past what are often called the garments of authority—the police uniform and badge, the doctor's white smock, the judge's robe, the pastor's frock and pulpit, the boss's title and corner office. For a large-scale society to work from day to day, we need to be able to believe that the people who have obtained their authoritative position will use the accompanying power wisely. As the following capsule stories demonstrate, however, there are many times when authoritative power is abused.

In 1963 Birmingham, Alabama, police commissioner Bull Connor used fire hoses and police dogs to repel peaceful civil rights demonstrators. Connor could get away with his behavior because he was the commissioner.

In March 1991 Los Angeles police officers chased and stopped Rodney King and his passenger, beat them fifty-six times with a baton, and kicked them six times, producing eleven skull fractures and brain and kidney damage. Citizens watched while the officers beat the two victims because the men in uniform were police.

Jim Jones, a fundamentalist cult leader, in 1978 relocated his Peoples Temple to 4,000 acres of jungle in Jonestown, Guyana, and led over nine hundred of his followers, including over two hundred children, to ingest a poisoned grape drink and commit mass suicide. The congregants followed Jim Jones because he was their religious leader.

In 2001 Dr. Thomas Theodore of Forestdale, Massachusetts, convicted of nine counts of mail fraud and three charges of violating the federal Food, Drug, and Cosmetics Act, was sentenced to 121 months in prison and a fine of $1.5 million in restitution to his victims. The evidence at his trial proved that Theodore and another businessman had managed to convince investors to give them $2 million, claiming they had discovered a promising cancer drug, LK-200, which, because the U.S. Food and Drug Administration had not approved it, would have to be produced outside the United States. In fact, it was not a new drug, it was not produced in a foreign country, and it had a questionable record in cancer treatment. The investors trusted Dr. Theodore, in large part, because he was a doctor.

In 1972, during the presidency of Richard Nixon, five men, at least one employed by the Committee to Re-elect the President, broke into the headquarters of the Democratic National Committee in the Watergate apartment complex in Washington, D.C., searching for campaign secrets. Why did the men follow such orders? Because they believed the orders had the tacit, if not explicit, blessing of the most powerful man in America, if not the world, the president of the United States.

In the late 1990s and early 2000s business leaders such as Jeffrey Skilling of Enron, Martin Grass of RiteAid, and John Rigas of Adelphia Cable, carried out dubious business schemes, stock maneuvers, and unorthodox accounting procedures, designed to create falsely positive numbers for their companies and/or personal gain. Members of their management teams and/or boards acquiesced simply because each of these executives was "the boss."

***Balancing Authoritative Power*** Once you realize that a Simply Difficult person is using authoritative power against you, you must find a way to balance the power. The good news is that, as explained earlier, just by taking the rational stance of asking the question, you have already begun this process.

Simply Difficult people commonly use authoritative power to end discussions before they even start. People are often so intimidated by another person's position or title, they do not dare ask for what they want. For instance, many lower-level accountants might

keep quiet if their chief financial officer told them that their concerns about the firm's accounting were unfounded. Residents who
were concerned about pollution in their neighborhood typically
would not challenge the head of the E.P.A. if he said "Everything
is okay." Often patients do not seek a second medical opinion because "the doctor said so," even when they have nagging doubts
about their prognosis.

Fortunately, many people do question authority and refuse to
give in or give up when someone in a power position issues "the
answer." Remember the reference to the chief executive officers
(C.E.O.s) who abused power? Here's an abridged version of what
happened to one of those bosses.

## THE DRUGSTORE DESPOT
### *Prescription for Disaster*

Impatient with his father at the helm of the RiteAid chain, Martin
Grass bullied Dad out of the C.E.O. position and took it himself.
(Actually, even before that step, he had already relentlessly pushed
his own brother aside.) Once in the job, he seemed to listen to no
one (except his cadre of sycophants), building new stores and gut-
ting old ones, spending lavishly on ad campaigns, buying up other
chains, all at a pace one might question based on what revenues
justified, but appearing to be a genius judging by his report card
of record profits.

However, it turned out the financials weren't real. They fell
apart under scrutiny. There were inconsistencies. Omissions. Outright errors. Even fabrications. As a public company, the stockholders were entitled to challenge him. And they did just that.

But Grass defied them. To him, they could not question his authority. This was his company. He inherited it from his father fair and square.

Even when he could hold the stockholders at bay, the government wanted an accounting. He defied them too, refusing to open his books. Some of his key employees began to admit things weren't right. Grass fired them. It seemed he was all-powerful. No matter how financially unsound or unjustified his dealings, he couldn't be stopped. Or so it seemed to Grass, members of his management team, and some of the board's directors.

But finally his house of cards began to crumble. The stockholders and the Securities and Exchange Commission (S.E.C.) set out to (1) *Ascertain* his source of raw power, including his corporate title, his holdings, and his intimidating style; (2) *Balance* his power with their own by the combined voting power of the public shares, which actually far outnumbered his, plus S.E.C. regulations, and the threat of cooperative employees who didn't want to be part of his renegade regime; and (3) *Communicate* the logical consequences of a showdown. If he didn't cooperate, he would face legal challenges, loss of power, fines, and possible imprisonment.

Grass ignored the consequences, and in the end his raw power disintegrated. The board, including his own family's representatives, voted to oust him. (His father and brother were long since lost as allies.) The government then prosecuted Grass. Then the final consequence occurred. Rather than face the verdict of a jury, Grass filed a plea agreement on charges of conspiracy to fraud and obstruction of justice and was sentenced by the judge to prison.

Although this example is compelling, such stories too often prove the exception rather than the rule. Most people see others in a position of authority and think that it is not within their own power to question that authority. However, as has been demonstrated, the best, most effective, field-evening way to balance someone's authoritative power is simply to question it.

> *"Why do you say what you say?"*
> *"Are you sure?"*
> *"What data back up your position?"*
> *"What are the alternatives?"*
> *"Does everyone agree with you?"*
> *"Have you considered the opposite view?"*
> *"What if we don't do what you want?"*
> *"What do other experts say?"*

Unfortunately, questioning authoritative power alone may not be enough. As we said earlier, most Simply Difficult people have more than one source of power. Even if you are able to balance their authoritative power, you are likely going to have to deal with that person's punishment power.

*Punishment Power*  In essence, punishment power is the power to take away something that matters to another person or to which the other person may even feel entitled. A client can punish vendors by canceling a huge contract. A supervisor or manager can punish a subordinate by cutting or refusing to pay a bonus. A parent can punish a teenager by taking away driving privileges. A blackmailer can threaten to reveal (or take away the secrecy of) someone's personal indiscretion. A superpower nation can cut off oil, military support, or loans to a smaller country unless that country goes along with the power's policies. And often, the Simply Difficult person can get his or her way without even making the threat, but just by having the reputation for using punishment power. The fear, based on past behavior, can be enough to intimidate others into compliance, to back down rather than stand and fight for what they want. Here's a story of how fear of what could happen resulted in high-performance behavior.

## THE WORLD SERIES OF HOTEL SERVICE

In the days before the 1994 baseball walkout, most of us on the inside of the game knew that though not yet called, a strike was a high probability and we knew the damage it could do. In an effort to discuss the issues and possibly even find alternatives that would avoid a strike, several team owners, executives, and player agents met in private. Not only was this our livelihood, but we all shared a true love of the game. It *was* our lives. We wanted the game to go on . . . and on. It was a tense, delicate, and very critical moment, and we all understood the implications of our decisions.

George Steinbrenner, renowned owner of the New York Yankees, offered to host the meeting at his own Tampa, Florida, hotel. Of course, Steinbrenner has a reputation that is larger than life, to say the least: He's wealthy. He spends fortunes on good ballplayers. He has a low tolerance for anything but winning. He's quick to fire anyone he feels isn't doing his or her best. He can be volatile. And he is passionate about competition. It's all true and it's all part of the legend. George Steinbrenner is every one of the descriptions above, and yet every one has been exaggerated to make for colorful news copy. He is, above all, good press. Where does the reality end and myth begin? It's hard to say. Both have contributed to his and the Yankees' success. Personally, many of my cohorts and I have always found him to be a first-class "good man."

At the prestrike meeting, George was nothing but gracious. His hospitality was first rate, and his generosity was genuine. The evidence of his thoughtfulness and sensitivity contradicted his baseball reputation as a punisher. In fairness, though, I have never been subject to his punishment power. Rather, as an agent representing ballplayers—ballplayers he wanted and needed—I was able to neutralize his ability to have punishment power over me. That day in Florida, to his guests, George Steinbrenner was the consummate host.

However, all of his guests, including me, could not help but notice the overt nervousness of Mr. Steinbrenner's hotel staff as they carried out their duties. From the moment waitstaff, attendants, or assistant managers tentatively entered the conference room until they subserviently backed out of the room, we could feel the tension rise. The servers' apologetic interruptions— "Excuse us, Mr. Steinbrenner . . ." "Sorry, Mr. Steinbrenner . . ." "Is this what you ordered, Mr. Steinbrenner?" "Can we get anything else, Mr. Steinbrenner?"—made the anxiety in the room palpable. The sweat beads on the staff's foreheads were visible, and dripping. We may have been in Florida in the summer, but the air-conditioning was firing out frosty air. The room wasn't hot; the bodies of the servers were on fire from the inside out. These people simply knew, in their bones, and perhaps in their collective experiences, but clearly by reputation, this man—Mr. Steinbrenner of the New York Yankees—had an expectation of excellence. And he would exercise punishment power should the standard of excellence fail to be met. If he would fire a major-league general manager for finishing second, why not a young man pushing a room-service cart? This may not have been the World Series, but to the staff it was the championship of meetings. Like his ballplayers, they wanted to perform perfectly, to impress him, to rise to his standards. And they were fearful of anything but.

This was punishment power not meted out but existing in its potential. It was there, in the atmosphere, affecting performance, without ever having been actually used. Every employee—like a designated hitter in a clutch situation—who stepped into that room knew they would either survive or perish, live up to perfection or fall short. Every employee—like a Gold Glove fielder, home run hitter, twenty-game winner, or general manager—was replaceable. There's another one just waiting for the chance to show what he's got.

Is this exaggeration? Of course. But remember, George Steinbrenner is a man who is larger than life. His legend is as powerful as his reality.

Baseball's leading owners, executives, and agents exhaustively explored the complexities and intricacies of economics, psychology, and business, in an effort to prevent the ultimate game delay. Meanwhile, there was another instructive dynamic at work in our midst—witnessing how punishment power, employed, threatened, or simply existent by reputation, can determine behavior.

In the end, we were not successful in averting the strike. But when baseball did resume the next year, look what happened. Buck Showalter, the Yankees manager who had been the Manager of the Year in the strike year of 1994, led the Yankees to a second-place finish in 1995. He was fired and replaced with Joe Torre for the 1996 season, in which, by the way, the Yankees won the World Series. And one has to wonder whether at the end of 1995 some good, but not good enough, members of the hotel staff might have been replaced with even better staffers for 1996.

* * *

Is George Steinbrenner larger than life? Yes. Does punishment power work? Yes. How do you overcome it? That's next. Right after an insight on premeditated punishment power.

*Insight:* Punishment power is often premeditated. Many Simply Difficult people plan their punishment strategy far in advance of any encounter. They set their trap by seeming to give their potential victims something and then subsequently threatening to take it away. This takeaway routine is particularly effective because people tend to overreact when they feel that something that is already theirs may be removed or retracted or repossessed. "Hey, wait! You can't have that. It's mine. You already agreed to give it to me. Now what do I have to do to keep it?"

One truly unscrupulous person we've encountered described with delight how he used this technique, which he called "getting them pregnant." He said he would promise almost anything to get the other side to say yes to a deal, and then once they had accepted—now "pregnant" with his promises—he would begin to gain concessions by brazenly taking back specifics he had promised. He found that people took ownership of deal points as if they were entitled to them, clung to them, and were even willing to trade off valuable points they wanted in order to keep points he had given them. When he negotiated this way, he bragged that he lost nothing but what he had already given. And he gained back a great deal. He gloated that it was like playing Las Vegas with the house money.

Yes, punishment power can work. But it can be counteracted.

*Balancing Punishment Power* The single most effective way to balance punishment power is to create a strong alternative. It is very difficult to punish people when they can escape the punishment or find an alternative to it. What if you didn't have to partner with that person who has such power over you? What if you were not under the thumb of that abusive boss? Or what if you actually had offsetting punishment power to that which is being held over your head? What if you too held the threat of punishment? That's balancing punishment power.

You do not necessarily have to achieve total control over the punisher, only the ability to either escape or to reverse the punishment. The other side simply has to be aware that you have such options and that you might use them. That, in itself, is often enough to balance the scales. Mark's story, which follows, involves a restaurant on the verge of demise, surrounded by potential punishment, with no way out . . . or so it seemed.

### PUNISHMENT FOR TWO
*A Recipe for Balance*

I was asked to help the owner of a prestigious restaurant—let's call it Le Bistro—that, unbeknownst to its upscale clientele, was in deep trouble. Ironically, their reservation book was always filled, the bar was doing standing-room-only business, and the chef's reputation was enviable. The problem was that Le Bistro's owner knew a lot more about food than he knew about the basics of business. As a result, Le Bistro's cost structure and cash flow were terrible. The rent was too high. The decor had cost a fortune. The wine cellar was extravagant. For several years, the restaurant had been bleeding red ink and had survived only through the owner's pledging his own home as collateral and through the constant infusion of capital from loyal, haute cuisine customers/investors, protecting their stomachs with their wallets.

Finally, the problem became too severe for even the most

dedicated gourmet angels. Le Bistro was behind in its rent as well as payments to suppliers. Its vendors threatened to cut off their renowned special cuts of meat, just-caught seafood, and superb, fresh produce. The landlord wanted his due; the bank, as primary lender, was demanding loan repayment; and the restaurant's daily payroll was in jeopardy. It was only a matter of time before word leaked out to the public and the once-in-demand hot spot would become poison. There was an interested buyer, a national restaurant investor group that wanted to add this regional jewel to its crown but only as long as the reputation remained untarnished.

At first glance, it seemed like everyone *but* Le Bistro's owner had punishment power. The private investors had long since run out of appetite for further bailouts. The landlord was prepared to evict. The bank was ready to retract the line of credit at a moment's notice, halting payroll and sending the high-profile personnel—waitstaff, wine steward, and maître d'—out on the street to spread the bad word. The suppliers—meat, fish, vegetables, wine, desserts—were poised to cut off the flow of goods and literally shut the kitchen down. And the buyer was willing to accept a damaged reputation as an excuse to drastically slash the purchase price.

What could Le Bistro and its owner do? This company had not just one bully with punishment power; it had an onslaught. Or so it would seem.

Until we took a step back to assess how we might balance the punishment power. Did we possess power we had overlooked? Could we offset their power? How might our side punish theirs? If one or more of the punishment alternatives came to pass, Le Bistro and perhaps even its owners could be forced to file bankruptcy, or a group of creditors could file an involuntary bankruptcy against Le Bistro. But that punishment worked both ways. Yes, the owner could lose his home and the investors their cash, but the bank would likely see only $.20 on the dollar. Their $2 million loan would collect, at best, $400,000, *if* the bankruptcy went smoothly, but likely it would be a lot worse. Did the bank want to be faced with a loss of well over $1.5 million? The vendors, if paid at all, would get a few pennies on the dollar and they'd be faced with no future business. The vendors knew that restaurants rarely actually reorganize under bankruptcy; the fallout of the publicity is too great, and haute cuisine customers are nothing if not snobbish and fickle. As for the prospective buyer, if Le Bistro went into bankruptcy, it might get a favorable price, but would the goodwill it'd be buying be worth anything? Or the buyer could be faced with a bankruptcy auction designed to drive the price as high as possible, get caught up in the "auction mentality," and overpay for a restaurant with little remaining goodwill. Bankruptcy was truly a double-edged sword.

We encouraged the owners to let it be known that bankruptcy was a real option *unless* more favorable terms could be worked out. Maybe the bank could renegotiate the loan, lengthening the term, and accepting interest-only payments in the interim. Maybe the vendors, if promised exclusivity as suppliers, would be willing to forgive some back payments and work out a reasonable ongoing payment schedule. Maybe the potential buyer, if given a guaranteed not-to-exceed sale price, could make advance payments on the purchase to relieve some of the investor debt. If all of those pieces fell into place, the bank would have a more secure client, payroll would be uninterrupted, and food quality would remain high; therefore, the clientele would remain loyal, and the new buyer would be taking over a healthy establishment, reputation intact.

Once we explained those realities to the other parties, in very blunt terms, that's just what happened. What seemed like one-sided punishment power wasn't. The threat of bankruptcy balanced that power. The business survived. The investors were unharmed. The owner sold Le Bistro, didn't lose his home, and gained a real education in how to run a business . . . for his next restaurant.

We aren't recommending you always call your opponent's bluff or opt for the most onerous solution. But we are suggesting you always step back from your situation, assess the threatened punishment from your adversary, and see if there isn't harsh medicine involved for both sides. See where the other side will be vulnerable, what might hurt them as well as you, what escape or alternatives you have to the sword they're dangling over your head. More often than we think, there is a balancing or offsetting action that has temporarily eluded us.

### When you feel you have no alternatives, get a second opinion

Of course, some people, in some instances, do not have access to such clear alternatives. They may not have the ability or option to walk away, nor can they employ a field-leveling device. A spouse may be in an abusive marriage that she cannot leave because of the children or for financial reasons. An employee may not currently have a job alternative when being mistreated by a boss. A company may be held hostage by a single-source supplier because there are no other qualified suppliers currently available in the market.

If you find yourself in a situation where there is no immediate, clear, and open alternative, we suggest that you begin to methodically work on creating a longer-term plan that will eventually create that alternative. Your own assessment may be dire. You feel there's no way out. No wonder; you're the one who's been trapped.

Go outside yourself. Get an objective opinion from a friend, a co-worker, or a deal coach, and you will often discover that you have much more at your disposal than you first thought. Perhaps the other party has money, but you have the goods, or vice versa. Maybe you have knowledge that has value or you have potential allies. You have the power to wait out the other person. You can walk away and take the loss or temporary setback. You could even call his or her bluff. These alternatives may not be readily found, easily implemented, immediately available, and they may not even be as attractive as the current situation. But they are real alternatives. It is hard work to overcome a Simply Difficult person who can cause you economic, emotional, and personal harm or loss. Rather than spending time lamenting your disadvantage, it is more productive to spend your time finding or creating viable alternatives to eliminate the Simply Difficult person's monopolistic advantage. Merely possessing the alternative allows you to reduce the threatened fear of manipulation by the Simply Difficult person.

*Resource Power* Many Simply Difficult people can bully others because of the sheer clout or power of the resources available to them. They have more money, more information, more people, more prestige, more time, and more influence than their counterparts (or, more appropriately, their victims) ever will. It can feel and in fact be overwhelming when facing an individual or entity that seems to hold all of the resource cards. Consider these examples of seemingly insurmountable resource power:

| ENTITY/INDIVIDUAL | RESOURCE POWER |
|---|---|
| George Steinbrenner and the Yankees | Owner with bottomless checkbook, most talented team in baseball |
| Michael Eisner and Disney | Turned Disney from cartoons to media-leisure conglomerate |
| Wal-Mart | Largest retail chain in the world |
| Elvis | Biggest star in history of music |
| Coca-Cola | Most popular soft drink worldwide |
| McDonald's | World's largest fast-food chain |
| United States | Most powerful economic/ military force on the globe |

While it may seem that one individual or entity has all the resources and attendant power, there is always an offset or a "but" that tends to make the world and life a little more fair.

| ENTITY OR INDIVIDUAL | RESOURCE POWER | BUT . . . |
|---|---|---|
| George Steinbrenner and the Yankees | Owner with bottomless checkbook, most talented team in baseball | Lost the 2003 World Series to Florida Marlins with lower-paid team |
| Michael Eisner and Disney | Turned Disney from cartoons to media-leisure conglomerate | Roy Disney and other board members forced Eisner's resignation |
| Wal-Mart | Largest retail chain in the world | Here comes Target, capitalizing on neglected "taste" market |

| ENTITY OR INDIVIDUAL | RESOURCE POWER | BUT . . . |
|---|---|---|
| Elvis | Biggest star in history of music | . . . until the Beatles |
| Coca-Cola | Most popular soft drink worldwide | Plain old water, not Pepsi, has stolen share from the giant |
| McDonald's | World's largest fast-food chain | Fast wasn't enough, and fat-consciousness, variety, and freshness led to rise of Subway and other challengers and to the loss of profits |
| United States | Most powerful economic/ military force on the globe | Even the United States is vulnerable to terrorism, needs worldwide support, allies in Iraq, and U.N. backing |

Even seemingly impervious forces are vulnerable to a balancing of their resource power. For virtually every resource of power, there is another resource that is perhaps less obvious, hidden, or not yet discovered but, once tapped, can offset and perhaps overcome the impervious person or entity. It's a matter of opening our minds and imaginations to finding that offsetting resource.

Resource power can be blunted. Not with just more of the same resource that is being used against you, but with imaginative, smart, alternative resources.

**Balancing Resource Power** When balancing resource power, there are two options: obtaining allies to match their resources, or focusing your resources. Let's consider *obtaining allies* first.

What most people never think about is that there are likely to be many others—other forces, schools of thought, or individual minds—who are also suffering at the hands of the resource-laden Simply Difficult person. Finding and working with those potential allies is a highly effective way to balance the other side's resource power.

---

### 13 COLONIES VS. THE BRITISH EMPIRE

*We must all hang together, or most assuredly,*
*we shall all hang separately.*

Ben Franklin to John Hancock at the
signing of the Declaration of Independence

---

In business, it's the principle that retail buying and merchandising groups like Epic Pharmacies have assembled, creating a confederation of independent drugstores banded together to market successfully against chains like Walgreens, CVS, and RiteAid. Or it's what local banks do in various local markets, sharing advertising costs by creating one ad campaign featuring a famous star and then customizing the campaign per geographic region. It's why airlines share frequent-flier miles. And it's why ATM machines accept each other's credit or debit cards. A classic example was when the six cast members of the hit show *Friends* decided early on to negotiate in concert for the same salary per star rather than as individual stars whom the network would eventually pit against one another. There's strength in numbers, especially in a world filled with giants, where some of those giants are Simply Difficult. A team is simply more powerful than an individual.

Speaking of teams, here is an out-of-the-ordinary application of the idea of finding allies. A truly mind-changing explanation of this premise was put forth by author Michael Lewis in his best seller *Moneyball*. He tells the story of Billy Beane, general manager of the Oakland A's, an underfunded major-league team, seemingly destined to be an also-ran to the deep-pocketed clubs who can literally "buy" stars and championships, until they found the most unlikely of allies—statisticians. As someone who has spent a large part of his life in and around professional baseball, Ron could relate directly to Lewis's book and its controversial premise.

## WHO CARES ABOUT R.B.I.S?

### *How* Moneyball *Changed the Paradigm in Major-League Baseball*

When I picked up *Moneyball*, I thought, "Finally someone has taken a long-overdue, truly fresh look at the game and how it works." What I didn't anticipate was how far and wide the ideas and concepts in the book would resonate, well beyond baseball.

On the surface, *Moneyball* is the story of Billy Beane's tradition-shattering approach to professional baseball. Essentially, he has embraced some long-standing, but largely ignored, theoreticians and statisticians—baseball nerds who don't play the game but instead study it with a lab scientist's intensity. They had taken a coldly analytical look at baseball and determined that the wrong stats were often used to measure and predict success. The time-honored runs-batted-in (R.B.I.s) statistic was a prime culprit. Billy and his cadre of iconoclasts maintained that R.B.I.s were a measurement of chance occurrences, that is, when players happened to be on base when a batter happened to get a hit. The batter had nothing to do with putting the runner on base. What was and is important is whether that batter is prone to get hits. And the experts even disproved that there is such a thing as a clutch hitter. The best hitters in baseball, statistically, hit the same in critical situations as they do in unpressured situations.

Stat by stat, Billy and his unlikely allies have taken the game apart and put it back together based on numbers and figures that *do* translate to hits and runs, not to mention strikes and outs. They found that fielding and pitching performance are much more important than most clever offensive maneuvers like the squeeze play and the bunt. They discounted the value of steals and discovered the neglected value of walks. Steals don't translate to runs. Walks do.

But the most important aspect of what Billy Beane did was *why* he did it. He had to in order to offset resource power. He had been the general manager of the Oakland A's, a club with one of the smallest budgets and payrolls in the major leagues. He had to go up against clubs with almost unlimited bank accounts, who could buy the best players, pay the biggest bonuses, pick up the most expensive free agents, and assemble a team of superpaid superstars that could thrash most of the other teams. How could the A's compete with the Yankees or Red Sox? How could they even compete across the bay with the San Francisco Giants? They had to be smarter, because they couldn't be richer. They had to find players that performed on criteria the rest of baseball was ignoring. And they have done it. In 1998, the year Beane became general manager, the team finished fourth in the West Division. In 1999 they finished second. In 2000 they were first, in 2001 second, and in 2003 first again. Year after year, with paltry-by-comparison payrolls, they have been a contender and a playoff team. Money met the statisticians and the statisticians were money's match—so much so that the Boston Red Sox (and several other teams) have adopted a similar approach.

But, as I said earlier, the impact of *Moneyball* has gone far beyond the ballpark. I know of C.E.O.s in major companies, professors at prestigious universities, and weekend golfers who have altered their analysis of what works and why, rejecting conventional wisdom and demanding that statistics be meaningful.

Close to home, my own son, Mark Shapiro, general manager of the Cleveland Indians, took the controversial tack of dismantling his team, trading away seeming stars (by old standards), and rebuilding from the ground up based on his own formula—not the same as Billy Beane's but certainly tradition-shattering, objective, and unjaded. Mark has tapped into his own set of unlikely, fresh-thinking allies to create a new kind of baseball team in Cleveland. And, with a father's pride, I say, it's working.

Now let's consider *focusing your resources.* Too often, when facing someone with superior resources, the tendency is to feel overwhelmed. You can't go toe to toe with someone who wears bigger, heavier, more expensive boots. You know you can't match dollar for dollar with someone with bottomless pockets.

One of the ways to deal with this situation is not to try. Don't match dollar for dollar or resource for resource or go toe to toe. You will lose. Instead, when you are overmatched, your only wise choice may be to find your best (or only) strength. Determine the other side's pressure points or vulnerabilities. All parties have them, even those who seem impervious. Search until you determine where your strength coincides with one of their pressure-point weaknesses. Then dedicate your energy to exploiting this opportunity, no matter how large or small, no matter the particular issue, but with the realistic goal of winning one, identifiable battle. Why? Because one well-chosen battle can turn the tide in an entire war.

Here is a business-sports-and-personal-story combination that shows how, against the odds, the ability to focus your resources can offset and balance enormous resource power.

### FREE AGENTS ALWAYS GO FOR THE MONEY . . . OR DO THEY?
*Balancing Resource Power in the N.B.A.*

I was asked to address the staff of the front office of an N.B.A. team on the principles we teach for business relations and deal making—in particular, how to contend with adversaries who can drastically outspend you. Following our session, I was contacted by the team's coach, one of the most respected and successful in pro basketball, who said, "With all due respect to your philosophy, I've rarely seen a player *not* opt for more money." Though he qualified his statement with some technical exceptions, he conveyed to me something more pervasive—the commonly accepted league (and life) wisdom that the teams with the most money (i.e., resources) will get the best players.

You may be thinking to yourself, "Sure, like the Los Angeles Lakers . . ." However, because basketball has a salary cap, it's not actually the same teams each year with the most money (as in baseball with the New York Yankees). Rather, the teams with the least amount of already committed money will have the greatest amount of available money under the salary cap and, consequently, be able to spend the most on the high-profile free agents. But I understood the coach's point: resource power in the N.B.A. is real power, and he had rarely seen a team with less money able to balance the resource power of another team, with more money, in trying to acquire the same player.

This was critically important, because at the time the coach (whom I'll call Coach Wise) and I had the discussion, his team (let's call them the Family) was trying valiantly to re-sign one of its star players (call him Jr.), who was now a free agent. The problem was that there were a handful of other teams with more cap room and thus more resource power than Coach Wise's team. He wasn't just facing one adversary or just one resourcefully powerful opponent. He was surrounded by a virtual axis of resourcefully powerful opponents, each of which possessed greater resource power than the next. He was fearful that his team's inferiority to other teams' resources would surely prevent its rising star player from returning. Coach Wise was upset and outright angry at the whole process.

I have changed the players', coaches', and team names. Who knows who might be playing for or with whom someday, somewhere? Suffice it to say Jr., as an upcoming player, was one of the bright minds and stars behind the stellar backcourt of the Family's recent World Championship team. Arguably, at the time, Jr. could have been considered the most exciting player at his position in the N.B.A. and was on track to becoming an All-Star.

The Family's brilliant and strategic front office made clear that it would offer the player a new long-term contract beginning the next season with a significant increase . . . very significant. That would have been the end of the process had it not been for the seller's market in which they were dealing. Even though some of the well-heeled contenders fell away, one very bold, very aggressive, very brash challenger emerged. From among the axis of resourcefully powerful teams, one team in particular—The Moguls—emerged as the primary competition to the Family. The Moguls not only had incredible resource power (the most in the N.B.A.) but also threatened to wield that power irrationally.

Recognizing Jr.'s exciting playmaking skills and ability to wreak havoc on opponents' defenses, the Moguls, desperately longing for a championship, set out to acquire his services for many future seasons, literally at all costs. They had much more salary cap room—that is, money—than any other team, and they were itching to spend it. The Moguls issued a virtual engraved invitation to Jr.: "We've opened our vault. Just back your truck in and load up."

The Family knew it needed to do something other than match the likely ridiculous offer from the Moguls. But how could they combat the deep pockets of the Moguls, especially if Coach Wise was right in believing that "money talks" and always wins?

The Family wasn't going to go toe to toe with the Moguls and spend dollar for dollar. After all, the Moguls outmatched the Family with available dollars, and everyone knew it. The Moguls simply had much more resource power. The Family had to brainstorm how to balance that resource power without battling against it and/or succumbing to it. Team managers came up with an idea. Instead of using dollars as their weapon, they decided to use something else, the one strength they had that no other team had, especially the Moguls—their intangibles. As a rising star, Jr. loved his role on the team, loved his community, and greatly appreciated the opportunity the Family had given him to play for a perennial contender. The cohesiveness and brotherhood of the team, its recent championship, and the team's deep, profound history and relationship with the player and his wife would/could/might protect the Family against the Moguls' exorbitant green . . . or would it?

If the Moguls team was going to lure him, it would have to offer something that would exceed the valuable relationships he built in the Family's hometown. The Moguls' solution, like that of many Simply Difficult people with abundant resources, was to irrationally and obscenely flaunt the most powerful abundant resource—cold, hard cash.

Given the emotional and financial pressure that was building, young Jr. had periodic conversations with another confidant, the general manager of the Family—we'll call him Mr. G.—with whom Jr. had built a real friendship. Mr. G. told Jr. how much he meant to the franchise and to Mr. G. personally. They shared not only coaching and playing history, championship games, and a close friendship, but Mr. G. had scouted and recruited Jr. seven years earlier when he was a gangly nineteen-year-old wannabe basketball player and then had drafted him five years later. The two had grown together, had seen each other's careers blossom, and had won together. Mr. G., head of one of the most truly caring front offices in the N.B.A., gave advice, not as to whether or not to visit other clubs and field other offers but rather as to what things Jr. should weigh in his decision-making process. Mr. G. described to the young player his own feelings about the importance of relationships. He talked about the realistic value, and sometimes overvaluation, of money. In the end, Mr. G. told Jr. that he would have to balance all of the factors—the two organizations, the relationships, the potential for growth and championships, the dollars, and his family's happiness.

The Family's management, having decided to focus their resources, agreed on one thing: If the relationships they'd built and valued with Jr. wouldn't bring him back and keep him, nothing would. How did they focus their resources? They used every opportunity to communicate with this young star how much they appreciated his efforts and his character. They enumerated the benefits of community, humanity, true team feeling, and personal relations as valuable, measurable assets, with as high a value as money.

Furthermore, the veteran superstar of the Family—whom we'll name the Prof—had developed a very close relationship with Jr. and, knowing Jr. was now a free agent, wanted his young cohort to stay. In fact, the Prof, while on vacation, phoned the young free agent and communicated to him the importance of their relationship as well as what the Prof saw as Jr.'s substantial role on the team. That in itself was testimony to the strength and unity of the Family.

As decision day approached, the Family's staff made themselves available to Jr. to ease his concerns, answer his questions, and extend their unyielding appreciation for him and desire to have him back.

By the day's end, Jr. had two options from which to choose. He could (1) play for a team that could offer as much as seventy million dollars or (2) play for a team that could offer something closer to fifty million dollars but that was in a place that was home to his friends, in a truly caring and diverse community with rich history, a promising future, and where he had already begun leaving his legacy.

The Family couldn't match the seventy-million-dollar-offer. The team could only budget fifty million dollars and focus its resources to balance the Moguls' bullying pocketbook. The team knew it had all the intangibles the Moguls didn't, and it spent its time and effort on those. But after all the hard work the Family put in, and all the blood, sweat, and tears team members dedicated to retaining this one-in-a-million player, did it work?

Well, suffice it to say that the Moguls had to scrounge around for a Plan B (and throw their money at another free agent) while the Family secured a star player (and family member) for six more years. As for Coach Wise, well, he's a little less cynical about players' motives and willing to acknowledge that resource power doesn't necessarily mean all-powerful.

## Communicate Consequences

Okay, once you have thoroughly assessed the type or types of power being used, once you've done your best to find a way to balance the power, you now have the task of communicating to the Simply Difficult adversary this new balancing of power. Needless to say, the other person isn't likely to accept the redefined balance with open arms. It is important, therefore, to understand that *how* you communicate this message may be as important as the message itself.

There are two contrasting approaches to communicating consequences to the Simply Difficult person: the hot approach and the cool approach.

***The Hot Approach, or Meeting Power with Power*** Most people think that you need to meet power with power. Come on as strong as your adversary. Don't back down. If he yells, you yell. If he growls, you growl. Yeah? Oh, yeah! Who says? I says!

By way of example, think of the witness-stand confrontation written by Aaron Sorkin for the film *A Few Good Men.*

### "I WANT THE TRUTH" SCENE FROM *A FEW GOOD MEN*

A military prosecutor, Lieutenant Daniel Kaffee, played by Tom Cruise, is interrogating hard-bitten Marine lifer Colonel Nathan Jessep, played by Jack Nicholson. Kaffee is out to prove that Jessep issued the Code Red order, a punishment that ultimately killed a soldier named Santiago. Jessep is just as determined to live by the sacrosanct, unspoken principles of the military, a morality he doesn't have to justify to anyone. It's a true mano à mano battle.

*Jessep:* You want answers?

*Kaffee:* I think I'm entitled to them.

*Jessep:* You want answers?

*Kaffee:* I want the truth!

*Jessep:* You can't handle the truth! Son, we live in a world that has walls. And those walls have to be guarded by men with guns. Who's gonna do it? You? You, Lt. Weinberg? I have a greater responsibility than you can possibly fathom. You weep for Santiago and you curse the Marines. You have that luxury. You have the luxury of not knowing what I know: that Santiago's death, while tragic, probably saved lives. And my existence, while grotesque and incomprehensible to you, saves lives . . . You don't want the truth. Because deep down, in places you don't talk about at parties, you want me on that wall. You need me on that wall. We use words like honor, code, loyalty . . . we use these words as the backbone of a life spent defending something. You use 'em as a punch line. I have neither the time nor the inclination to explain myself to a man who rises and sleeps under the blanket of the very freedom that I provide, and then questions the manner in which I provide it! I'd rather you just said thank you and went on your way. Otherwise, I suggest you pick up a weapon and stand a post. Either way, I don't give a damn what you think you're entitled to!

*Kaffee:* Did you order the Code Red?

*Jessep:* I did the job you sent me to do.

*Kaffee:* Did you order the Code Red?

*Jessep:* You're goddamn right I did!

Kaffee demands. Jessep retorts. Kaffee is relentless. Jessep unleashes a diatribe. Kaffee pushes Jessep to the edge. Jessep teeters. Kaffee goes for the kill. Jessep confesses. Kaffee outmachos his supermacho foe. Yes, it happens, but not often. And you never know who really is the strongest, the most powerful, the most determined, in the end.

**The Cool Approach, or Staying Calm and Collected but Powerful**
Some situations do call for the blunt approach described above. But the second method, the one we typically recommend, is taking a cooler, more calculated approach. Be calm, be confident, be in control. Let your counterpart know that you have balanced the power, but let him or her know in a way that not only communicates but lets him or her think hard about the consequences of new balance.

By way of example, think of another film scene, this one from *Sudden Impact.*

### "DO YOU FEEL LUCKY?" SCENE FROM *SUDDEN IMPACT*

Dirty Harry, played by Clint Eastwood, has chased a lowlife, who has tried to kill Harry. Finally, Harry has the thug cornered, but not until after having fired a lot of shots from his gun. The cornered man has to decide if Harry has any bullets left. Should he run? Should he give up? Harry, very coolly, communicates the new balance of power:

> I know what you're thinking. Did he fire six shots or only five? Well, to tell you the truth, in all this excitement, I've

kinda lost track myself. But being as this is a .44 Magnum, the most powerful handgun in the world, and would blow your head clean off, you've got to ask yourself one question. Do I feel lucky? Well, do ya, punk?

Harry doesn't shout. He almost whispers. He doesn't brag that he has bullets left. In fact, he uses the unknown for its impact. Maybe he does. Maybe he doesn't. And he lets the real power sink in. Things are balanced now. What will you choose to do? We will discuss both approaches in detail.

*Natural Logical Consequences* First, the cooler, more calculated approach is based on communicating what we call natural logical consequences. This technique is a variation on the idea of wrapping an iron fist in a velvet glove. Gentle on the outside but firm on the inside. The message delivery may be soft and polite, but the power implied within that message is unmistakable. The listener then draws conclusions based on both the soft delivery and the clear inner message. They respond in a logical sequence. You carry the logic further by explaining what will naturally happen next.

Using this technique in response to the stance the Simply Difficult party has taken—Point A—you present your resulting position calmly and clearly—Point B, the natural consequence of Point A. In so doing, you are laying out a projection of the potential course of events. If the Simply Difficult person continues his unacceptable behavior, from B to C, it will only be natural for you to respond in a given, prestated manner sequence, from C to D and so on. Pretty soon, he will get the message. If he continues to respond predictably and negatively, he can expect an outcome that gets progressively worse, all the way to Point Z—not a place even the most Simply Difficult would wish to end up.

What is most important here is that rather than issuing a blatant threat that you will try to punish the other side, you are presenting a logical, almost undeniable sequence, one that the other side can hardly argue since he would do what you are doing were the roles reversed.

Typical phrases to use in communicating natural logical consequences include:

> *"I'm sure neither of us would want to . . ."*
> *"I would hope it would never go to the point where . . ."*
> *"I can see a domino pattern emerging . . ."*
> *"If you play this out, it isn't heading in a good direction for either of us . . ."*
> *"What I would like to avoid is . . ."*

The lesson of overcoming Simply Difficult people and balancing power by communicating natural logical consequences was indelibly etched on the minds of historians by the life led by the legendary leader Gandhi. His life and lessons were dramatized in the movie *Gandhi* and, in particular, in the scene summarized below. Needless to say, this was the ultimate "cool" approach.

## "IT'S TIME YOU LEFT" SCENE FROM *GANDHI*

Gathered around a conference table were the military and political leaders of the British Empire and India, including the viceroy, Lord Irwin, their staffs, and Mohandas Gandhi, the seeker of change through nonviolence. Gandhi, who exemplified communicating natural, logical consequences in a cool but pointed manner, had called the meeting to express his country's desire for independence from British rule. At the outset, Gandhi conveyed to Lord Irwin that the social and governmental problems had escalated beyond what could be handled through fiat or legislation. As Gandhi explained, his people had come to recognize that the British used intimidation and humiliation to exact the behavior they wanted from the Indians. This was intolerable to the very character of the Indian people. Gandhi, almost without a show of emotion, hands in his lap, voice even, uttered a simple sentence to Lord Irwin. "It is time you left."

Gandhi calmly went on to explain to Lord Irwin that whatever problems existed in India with respect to the religious minorities were just that, India's problems to deal with and solve, not England's. Solutions could not be imposed by heavy-handed rule. They must come from within the society.

In contrast to Gandhi's tranquil style, Lord Irwin's lieutenant, a textbook Simply Difficult type, responded with open hostility. He sarcastically challenged Gandhi, "How do you propose to make [those problems] yours [rather than ours]? You don't think we're just going to walk out of India?"

Gandhi replied to Lord Irwin (not to his abrasive lieutenant), "Yes, in the end, you will walk out." In a deliberate manner, absent any threat of violence or rancor, he elucidated, ". . . because 100,000 Englishmen simply cannot control 350,000,000 Indians, if those Indians refuse to cooperate. And that is what we intend to achieve—peaceful, nonviolent, noncooperation until you, yourself, see the wisdom of leaving, Your Excellency." Ever the polite gentleman, Gandhi continued to refer to Irwin by his title, even at a time of delicate confrontation.

Every gesture and every word was the embodiment of Gandhi wrapping his iron fist—the power and force of 350,000,000 Indians to resist and repel British rule—inside a velvet glove. The words were courteous and respectful, but they communicated a powerful position, that of noncooperation and potential rebellion.

Lord Irwin heard measured words but an unmistakably strong message. He recognized that Gandhi was spelling out the natural, logical consequences that would occur if the British did not leave India. He clearly understood that Gandhi's preview of the inevitable chain of events resulted then and there in a balancing of power. Lord Irwin, however he may have reacted on the surface, would forever after concentrate not on posturing or rebuttal, but on the reason and reasonableness of Gandhi's assertions.

If the British attempted to continue their choking control over India, it would only be natural for the Indians to respond with opposition. The British forces would then counter with a tighter stranglehold. That would be met with still more Indian opposition. Confrontation would lead to bloodshed. Bloodshed would lead to mass revolt. And in the end, 100,000 British troops would be trying to quell the fire of 350,000,000 Indians fighting for their very survival. Lord Irwin knew at that moment the power had shifted and would forever be balanced, if not tilted toward India.

*Going Nuclear . . . Carefully* Sometimes, not often, once in a while, occasionally, very occasionally, when nothing else works, you may have to go ballistic (but only if it's planned and controlled and only if absolutely nothing else works with your implacable, unreasonable, incorrigible adversary). In other words, don't use this hot approach unless you have to.

Okay, sometimes Simply Difficult people can only hear or pay attention to others when the others are screaming at the top of their lungs. With all of the caveats, warnings, and disclaimers we have given, we do believe that every once in a while, demonstrating some controlled rage can be effective.

The story Ron tells exemplifies such a rare instance.

## CONTROLLED RAGE
### *Use with Caution*

Early on a hot summer morning in July of 1983, on what was to have been the first day of my carefully planned vacation, I received a call from a local law enforcement officer. He was giving me advance warning that several Baltimore Orioles players, including one of my clients, had attended a party the previous evening that had been subject to police surveillance. The police, suspecting illegal drug use at the party, checked out their suspicions, and the officer indicated that as a result a news story containing the allegations would be breaking during the day. Day one of my vacation was hardly looking like a lounge in the hammock with a good book.

The first call I made was to notify Hank Peters, then Orioles general manager, of the impending news. We arranged for a ten o'clock meeting at his office in the old Memorial Stadium (deep in the bowels of the ancient stadium, hardly the surroundings in which you'd find baseball executives in this day and age).

During the meeting, Hank and I worked our way through secondhand stories, rumors, and facts, trying to get to the bottom of the allegations, trying to prepare for the dreaded story soon to be released. Prevention, or at least containment, of a publicity flare-up regarding our players was our first priority. After the first tidal wave, we would then deal with the "who," "what," and "how bad" aspects to follow.

At one point in the day, the local television news teams unexpectedly showed up at the stadium to conduct an investigative piece. This was before we even knew enough to respond accurately. One particular reporter shoved a microphone in my face with a pointed question about the players and drugs, assuming that a damning incident had taken place (which had not yet been proven and, in fact, would never be proven). I was angered at the inflammatory, irresponsible nature of the news coverage, the leap to assumptions of guilt, and, knowing of serious drug problems among on-air talent at that particular television station, I blunted the reporter's questions by countering, "If we're going to explore 'allegations,' maybe you'd like to talk about the drug allegations at your station." My answer evidently took the reporter and cameraman by surprise, because the next thing that happened was the lights went dark and the microphone was shut off. Unfortunately, that only quelled the media pursuit temporarily. Later that afternoon, I was contacted by a member of the F.B.I. I agreed to have my client cooperate and try to persuade other players to work with the authorities. It was a long, tough day. It was about to get tougher.

Around four-thirty, Edward Bennett Williams, the celebrated trial lawyer (so celebrated, he was known by his initials, E.B.W.) and then owner of the Baltimore Orioles, stormed into Hank Peters's office and began to take his anger out not only on Peters but also on me, perhaps as a symbol of representation of the players. He screamed, he slammed, and he hollered, not too far from my face, declaring that this was "the darkest day in the history of the Orioles' franchise." Unrelated to the alleged incidents at the party, yet no doubt an emotional factor in Williams's disposition, Tippy Martinez, the Orioles' star relief pitcher, had been rushed to the hospital with appendicitis earlier that day. Not only was his team under suspicion of drug use, but in the run down the stretch for the pennant, the immediate playing future of one of his premier players was in doubt.

Was E.B.W. always Simply Difficult or was he having a Simply Difficult bout? As one who came to know him well, I would say he was perhaps more prone to be Simply Difficult than your average easygoing, happy-go-lucky guy, but, like many Simply Difficult people, challenging circumstances brought on and exacerbated his most acute Simply Difficult symptoms. He was simply at his Simply Difficult worst.

After E.B.W. ranted and raved, I realized the only way I was going to balance his substantial power (and anger) was to communicate to him the consequences of his actions. I tried to communicate those consequences calmly and factually. He ranted louder and stronger. I patiently waited for him to run out of steam. When he took a breath, I tried again to firmly explain that if he took this volatile route, things would only escalate, the players would rebel, the media would feed on it, the players would fall apart singly and as a team, and, guilty or innocent, the fallout would continue for days and weeks, poisoning a potentially great season. I say that I *tried* to explain because I did not succeed. E.B.W. drowned me out by more ranting, raving, and railing (not the three Rs we teach). Finally, it became clear that I could clarify, elucidate, and enlighten until I was exhausted from being reasonable, and I still wouldn't be heard. The din of anger was overwhelming. And I wasn't the only target. Hank Peters had been verbally knocked from one end of the room to the other. We were bruised and battered by vitriolic words. There was nowhere to go but ballistic. But the thought flashed through my mind that I had to go "carefully ballistic." If ever there was an oxymoron, this was it. Controlled insanity. Logical irrationality.

I looked Edward Bennett Williams square in the eyes and,

with language I would never recommend or turn into a teaching tool, I released some of the most creative and colorful expletives I had heard over the course of my life in sports. Then I said (okay, shouted) to Williams that I was leaving and he could just handle the situation himself. I ripped the door open and then slammed it so hard as I exited, several of Peters's prized memorabilia and sentimental pictures crashed to the floor.

I walked deliberately (but not too fast) up the subterranean corridor. No more than thirty seconds later, I heard the heavy wingtips of E.B.W. chasing me down the hall, imploring me to return to complete my mission. He begged me to please come back and help salvage the dignity, image, and perhaps success of the Orioles for the remainder of the season, and maybe the future. I agreed (and breathed a secret sigh of relief that my ploy worked).

We all agreed to a calm and calculated plan after that. We spoke in one voice. We used measured tones and measured words with the media, with the law enforcement agencies, with the players, and with major league baseball officials. In the end, no Orioles player was arrested and none was found to have used drugs.

In fact, despite the drug allegations, and proof that the incident took no toll, the Orioles survived that "darkest day" and went on to win the 1983 World Series. And because I represented so many people on the team, and because of our strengthened relationship, Edward Bennett Williams, who not long ago had used me for verbal target practice, took me as his guest to Japan the following year for the Major League Baseball World Champion Team–Japan All-Stars Tour.

In this particular case the hot approach worked. But only as a last resort. Don't use it unless you have exhausted all other methods. And use it judiciously. Cautiously. Or did we mention that already?

## PART FIVE

# E—Explore Options

*Getting "Unstuck"*

# CHAPTER FOURTEEN

# Hey, Dad, I Have an Idea for My Punishment
*How to Turn Dead Ends into Detours*

## IF YOU CONTROL THE ENCOUNTER, WHY SHOULD YOU EXPLORE OPTIONS?

THE IDEA BEHIND controlling the encounter was to enable you to respond appropriately to each type of difficult person. If you are in control, you can shape the exchange and even the outcome. Instead of the other side controlling the encounter and, as a consequence, controlling you, you have learned to assess your counterpart, counter his or her tactics, and reverse the leverage. At this point, the circumstances should look like one of these scenarios:

- The Situationally Difficult person should be calmed to the point where he or she can consider rational solutions.
- The Strategically Difficult person's tactics should have been recognized, responded to, and redirected.
- The Simply Difficult person should realize that there is at least a balance of power, and therefore he or she may not be able to dictate all of the terms.

You have created a new paradigm by controlling the encounter. Emotions have been calmed, strategies have been neutered, and power has been balanced. You are now in a position to make meaningful progress with the other side. *But* that doesn't mean it will happen yet.

## A PLACE CALLED "STUCK" . . . AND HOW TO GET OUT OF THERE

Unfortunately, even after you have controlled the encounter with a Situationally, Strategically, or Simply Difficult person, you may still be stuck because of any of the following reasons:

> *They took a position . . . You took a position.*
> *They explained why their position was a must . . . You explained*
>     *why your position was a must.*
> *They won't budge . . . Nor will you.*
> *They want A . . . You want B.*

Now what?

Maybe the answer isn't A or B. Maybe it's C or D or M. Maybe the answer is an option that has not yet been considered. Not their position, but not yours either. Not black or white, but gray, a nuance no one had yet contemplated. When you learn to brainstorm options, you can get past the impasses of seeming "musts," the attitude of "winner take all," the fragility of egos, the embarrassment of losing face, the stubbornness of . . . stubbornness. Options allow the other side to choose from alternatives instead of giving in to only one choice (which, by definition, is not a choice).

> *Alternatives are the aspirin of fevered conflict.*
>
> James Dale

When two sides argue/deal/debate/negotiate/bargain to no avail—my way versus your way—often the answer is "ways" that haven't been considered, new solutions from new angles. The fresh alternatives or options lower the tension because they remove the ego issue of my idea versus yours and they offer a whole new manner and mind-set for thinking about the issues at hand.

If you learn how to tailor your responses per type of difficult person (as we did in the last chapter) and learn how to develop options (as we do in this chapter), then you can get unstuck.

## OPTIONS—THE DIFFERENCE BETWEEN DEAD ENDS AND DETOURS

If you drive down a highway and come to one of those big yellow signs that says "Stop! Road Ends," you have nowhere to go. You have to turn around and go back, something none of us likes to do, not only in driving but especially in life. If you're dealing with a difficult person and suddenly you reach a roadblock or dead end—"Stop! Deal Ends!"—it seems you have no choice but either to backtrack and give up ground or to scrap the deal altogether. On the other hand, if you drive down a road and come to a sign that says "Detour Ahead," you may be annoyed the trip is going to take longer, you may even get frustrated that your path is less direct, but you also know that the detour will enable you, eventually, to get to your destination. When you cannot (or will not) move forward because of an apparent roadblock, use your creativity and discover that new alternative—that new route, the detour.

Here is an example of a young—very young—N.I.C.E. practitioner who created his own detour to get around what otherwise would have been a familiar dead end. Mark tells the story of the young practioner, his own son, Jack, who found a creative way around a roadblock put up by none other than Mark himself. It proves you're never too young to come up with creative options.

## HEY, DAD, I HAVE AN IDEA FOR MY PUNISHMENT

My son, Jack, throughout his six-year career of negotiating (the same number of years he has been on earth, dealing with me and his mother), has learned—no, make that mastered—the art of creating options. As the firstborn, prince of the manor, and young master of all in his domain, Jack has endeavored to maintain dominance throughout our household, including threatening, scaring, and even "nudging" his little sister, Anna, demonstrating his own brand of difficult negotiator. Needless to say, when I learn of Jack's having run afoul of the house rules, I assume my protective and disciplinary parental role. (I'll show him who's prince of this manor, who runs this domain.)

Granted, my punishments for Jack are predictable (consistent, I like to say). And Jack's innate understanding of me is based on this predictability. It has contributed to his early ability to be creative in coming up with ideas and options. In other words, he knows just how I am going to punish him before I even do it. I will invariably send him to a "time-out," isolating him from television, toys, other kids, the computer, and so on. Much like Pavlov's dog, Jack has internalized the connection between misbehaving (terrorizing his sister) and an immediate time-out. In fact, he knows it so well that often, when Jack has done something he knows is wrong, before I can even issue my sentence, he will put himself in a time-out. Countless times, Anna will report (as younger siblings do) on Jack's latest transgression. I will call out for Jack, and the next thing I hear is his preemptive response, "I'm in time-out, Daddy!"

Evidently, after experiencing numerous time-outs, Jack decided that the time-out was worn out. He was tired of being isolated, cut off from life's finer things, and having no fun. He decided it was time to get around this detour and create an option for me, an alternative to the time-out.

When Jack committed his next (and inevitable) in-home offense, I of course called time-out for him. Instead of hearing the familiar and comforting, "I'm in time-out, Daddy," Jack walked right up to me and said, "Yes, Daddy?" I was surprised at Jack's temerity, his willingness to question the consequences. I was ready to make it very clear to Jack that he could not take advantage of his sister; it was not acceptable big-brother behavior, and he was in for another time-honored time-out.

Before I could issue the edict, Jack offered his creative option. "Daddy, I have an idea. Instead of going to time-out, what if I went to clean my room instead?" Though I was tempted to stick to the proven punishment of the time-out, I couldn't help but be proud of Jack's creativity in brainstorming his own punishment. I even rationalized that having Jack clean his room would actually be more of a lesson-teacher than standing idle in an empty room. He would be literally making amends. So, per Jack's creative alternative, I agreed to "punish" Jack with an afternoon of cleaning.

My wife, Lori, who had been out, returned home just after I

sent Jack to clean his room and asked why he was upstairs. I recounted the story to Lori, at which point she broke into laughter. "You're teaching him a lesson? That's what you call making him clean his room? I call it falling for his brilliant trick. I cleaned his room an hour ago. He's not up there cleaning and thinking about what he did wrong. He's playing with his toys and basking in the glory of putting one over on you!"

I couldn't really get mad. He was demonstrating just what we teach—creative options. But I could go up to his room, have a little talk, and suggest an immediate—you guessed it—time-out.

As illustrated in this little story (of how a six-year-old outfoxed his wise, old father), people sometimes feel they have limited or even no options. Until the little lightbulb clicked on, Jack knew only one ending to his bad behavior—a sentence of a time-out. But, as he proved, creating options can turn dead ends into detours, detours that take you out of isolation and into your room full of toys and games and computers. The route on the road of life—family, social, or business—may not be direct. It may be rocky, rutted, potholed, bumper-to-bumper, circuitous, mountainous, or long and not well marked (even blocked by Dad), but the persistent, imaginative navigator will get there.

> *I took the road less traveled by.*
> *And that has made all the difference.*
>
> Robert Frost

## A DILEMMA WITH NO GOOD ANSWER? OR . . . ?

Here's an example of a challenge that seems, at first, to have no ideal solution. You have three choices: A, B, or C. Each one has its merits, but you must make a choice. You cannot choose all three. To make matters worse, these choices don't involve objects or abstract ideas but rather people—living, breathing humans with vulnerabilities and feelings. So it seems no matter which person you satisfy, two will be hurt or angry or abandoned. If A wins, B and C lose. If C is picked, A and B are left out. If B is happy, A and C are miserable. And no matter what, it's your fault. It looks like there's just no good answer. But maybe this is because, at first, most of us look at the obvious solutions instead of the less conventional or imaginative solutions.

We use the little allegory that follows to show people how they can come up against an apparently impossible dilemma or dead end and, through creative thinking, find options or detours around the dilemma. Read it and see if you can come up with an option before you get to the end of the story.

## THE GUILT TRIP

You're driving along in your two-seater car on a windy, wet, cold, stormy night. Lightning flashes. Thunder crashes. Large dogs are blown across the highway like newspapers. You can barely navigate your way safely through this monsoon when you spot three people huddled at an unsheltered bus stop, shivering, soaking wet, waiting for what is obviously a very, very late bus. Through your overworked windshield wipers, you can ascertain the following: that Person 1 is a frail, aged lady who looks as if she is about to be swept away by the storm or, at the very least, come down with pneumonia; that Person 2 is an old and dear friend who once saved your life; and that Person 3 is that once-in-a-lifetime man or woman who, up to now, you have only seen in your dreams.

Which one would you choose to offer a ride, knowing that there can only be one passenger in your car (and why didn't you buy that minivan)? What are your options?

1. Choose the elderly lady, the one who is most in jeopardy to survive the night (but risk upsetting your lifelong friend and miss out on the chance to meet your one and only soul mate).

2. Pick your friend because he did once save your life and you vowed someday to repay him (but then you'll endure the eternal guilt of worrying that the fragile matron died, not to mention the anxiety of leaving the man/woman of your dreams stranded in the storm only to get a ride from the next passing potential soul mate).

3. You could follow your romantic instinct (cue the violins) and open your door (and your heart) to your true soul mate (while coldly turning your back on the defenseless old lady and your former best friend, now your newest enemy).

So there is no right answer, right? What do you do when confronted with a situation when none of the options seem to work, when, no matter what you do, you do the wrong thing? Answer: Create another option. Create an option outside of the three obvious options. Maybe there are four. Or five or six. Like what? Here's just one more idea:

4. Give your car keys to your old (trusted, reliable, lifesaving, safe-driving) friend, and let him drive the lady home or to the nearest hospital to make sure she's all right.

Then you could stay behind, enduring the frigid gales, torrential rains, and lightning bolts, alongside the man or woman of your dreams. What better way to get to bond with your soul mate than by braving the elements, huddled side by side, hand in hand, cheek to cheek . . . Well, you can take it from here.

While not immediately evident, this is a creative option that accommodates all of the people in the story. Instead of the expected solutions that, at best, have one winner and two losers, this option actually has three winners (or four, counting you). Did you come up with an option of your own before we got to ours? Did you think outside the confines of the expected and find a solution that served all three people without alienating one or two? There are actually countless possible ways to solve this dilemma, but they all require breaking the bounds of conventional thinking.

# CHAPTER FIFTEEN

# The Largest Contract for a TV News Anchor

*Why and How Options Work*

THERE ARE FOUR SOUND, sensible reasons why options can create movement where no progress previously existed:

1. *Exploring options signals cooperativeness, not necessarily weakness.* When two parties get stuck, one of them must make the first move to get unstuck. What many people fear is that by making the first move, they will be at a disadvantage, or at least be perceived by the other party to be at a disadvantage. Certainly, this could be the case if the first move made is a truly significant concession—giving up a key deal point, abdicating a long-held position, or sacrificing principles or goals. If, however, your making the first move is an icebreaking genuine effort to get additional options (choices, ideas, or new approaches) on the table, you can create movement without making (significant) concessions. Options help you get moving without giving in.

2. *Options open the other side to your ideas.* Often when you hit a roadblock, that roadblock has been constructed by the

other side. It says, in effect, "No! Go no further. Stop. Talk
to the hand. Finished. My way or no way." Your adversaries
aren't listening to you or your proposal. You made your
offer. They made theirs. They rejected yours. Now they're
suffering from severe tunnel vision and the only light they
see at the end of the tunnel is the illumination from their
own idea. However, if you can introduce an option or
multiple options, other than theirs and outside of your
previous offers, you may be able to open their minds. All it
requires is opening a sliver or a crack, just enough to let a
new thought in. They may now see a way to make a deal via
your options. Or your new options may lead to yet another
thought on their part, a permutation of your option
(perhaps one they can claim as their own). The point is that
you've bypassed a roadblock or taken a detour. And
remember, detours ultimately get you to your destination.
3. *Options give the other side the feeling of control.* Difficult
people are often people trying to gain or maintain control
of a circumstance. Ultimatums, demands, or nonnegotiable
points from your side seemingly take away control.
Difficult people react to threatened loss of control by
refusing to budge, once again creating an impasse. The
more they fear losing control, the more entrenched they
may become in their positions. What you want is to
introduce ideas to them that they will consider seriously. By
suggesting options or alternatives rather than just
presenting, or re-presenting, ultimatums, you allow your
difficult opponents to select the option they like best. They
are now looking down a menu at a choice of entrées,
instead of staring at a plate of food they don't like. They

don't have to swallow your ultimatums. More important, you have set the input (or the menu), determining which options you're open to, but because they have the freedom to select, they feel as though they've retained control.

4. *Options allow the other side to have a "win" and save face.* Generally speaking, difficult people are not looking for a win-win situation. (They are, after all, difficult, not reasonable.) Not surprisingly, their goal is a win for them. Period. They win and, as a consequence, you lose. Too bad for you. By developing options (again, other than your original stance or goal), you can often find positions or concessions that allow the other side to "win" without materially affecting your desired outcome. By giving up something that means little to you, you are symbolically granting the other side a perceived victory. They have a "win." (In their eyes, you may have a "loss." If that makes them feel better, great.) The deal is made and they save face. Remember, taking this approach does not mean that you give them everything they want just so they can save face. You give them what you choose to give them. You put points on the table that are less important to you but nonetheless represent a victory to the other side. And if you give them choices of points, each of which is okay for you to sacrifice, they will have a greater sense of a "win," while you ended up with a resolution that met your true needs. In other words, creating options is one way to help the other side to have it *your* way.

*Note:* When creating options in which you give up a point or points that are not critical to your position, obviously your concessions have to be realistic. You cannot give up frivolous or transparently meaningless points. You have to give up very real points but ones that, in the end, you would have been willing to sacrifice in order to achieve the core of your position.

## WRITING THEIR PRESS RELEASE

It can be challenging for most of us to come up with solutions that allow the other side to save face. Because it's hard to step outside of ourselves and think like the other side. (Hey, they are the other side. How could they be right?) One technique we have used to bridge the gap to their foreign territory is the exercise of "writing the other side's press release." In other words, as you come up with options that they may find attractive, give yourself the hypothetical assignment of crafting a statement to the press that explains why the resolution is a "win" for the other person, as if you are the other person. Forcing yourself to go through this exercise will ensure that you frame proposals or options from a point of view that demonstrates benefit to the other side. It is rare that you will ever be in a situation in which you are writing a real (not just hypothetical) press release. But once it did happen to Ron. He did actually write the press release to announce the other side's "victory" (which, in reality, he had shaped and defined on behalf of his client). It's a story that graphically demonstrates why options work and how to employ them to get out of a maze filled with apparent impasses.

## HOW A TV STATION BRAGGED ABOUT GIVING THE
## LARGEST CONTRACT EVER TO A NEWS ANCHOR
### Or Is the Wallet Half-Empty or Half-Full?

For some on-air talent, the television news business works like this: A local staff reporter works his or her way up the news shifts from crack-of-dawn to midday to evening news, from remote field assignments to regular beats to the anchor desk. At the same time, that reporter is hoping to work his or her way up the market ladder, from middle of nowhere to middle of somewhere to pretty big town to major-market metropolis, and maybe even to that hallowed place—the national network. Local-market television station general managers constantly study one another's on-air talent, raiding and wooing the best, with promises of greater exposure, better time slots, and more dollars. It all makes economic sense because local news is relatively inexpensive to produce and, if highly rated in the market, can generate very sizable revenue and bottom-line profit for the local station. The contract negotiations are not unlike those in major-league sports, give or take a few zeros.

I happened to represent a major-market television newscaster who found himself to be a very sought-after anchor. In fact, as the process unfolded, research revealed he was the single most desired local anchor in the country at the time. Lots of managers at lots of stations—in not just large, but the largest of markets, including the home markets of the networks—had been following his career. They knew he had led his local major-market station from the middle of the pack to a clearly dominant, almost untouchable, number one position. They knew that the station had enjoyed record ad sales and profits with this anchor at the eleven o'clock news desk. They knew what a strong lead-in he was to the late-night programming in which the station made even more ad revenues. These station managers know talent and they also know the industry, so they knew that this anchor's contract was coming up for renewal. They were poised and ready to pounce, klieg lights lit, anchor desks polished, piles of green bait in their traps.

Of course, our local major-market station manager knew that all the other station managers in the country were getting ready to court their star anchor. He knew some of those large markets could dangle brighter lights and bigger cities, more glitz, more glitter, and closer proximity to the network. Truth be told, in his most private moments, the local station exec thought he'd lost his number-one anchor.

Everyone seemed to know everything. Except one salient fact. The anchor didn't *want* to go anywhere. This market, this town, had become his hometown. It was big enough, the lights were bright enough, and he had long since lost any desire to be a network anchor; life was good. *But* he did want to be paid like the most sought-after anchor in the country.

So, in representing him, first I made the case for compensating him commensurate with what other stations in other major markets would pay. I studied his ratings during his time slots, how they had risen over time, how much his ratings outdistanced the direct competition, even how they compared with other like markets around the country. I looked at how his ratings impacted the ratings of the shows he led into and again compared with other lead-ins around the country that fell short of his performance. I looked at market research that clearly showed that he was not only the most recognized newscaster in the market, but the most trusted, best-liked, overall most credible. I looked at the station's ad revenues in total, specifically those for his newscasts and, again, how they had risen as his popularity had risen. This man, almost single-handedly, was bringing in record profits for the station. The station, on the strength of those record profits, as part of a national network, had become a star in the national constellation.

Certainly, the figures would show that they could afford to pay him a great deal more. But they would not want to significantly raise his pay only to have to go through this tortuous process at the end of his next short contract cycle. Would they then risk losing him after having spent a small fortune to keep him temporarily, losing valuable time they might have invested in developing his successor? They would have to feel they could tie him up with a long-term commitment and assure themselves of not having to go through this process again.

To their happy relief, since his personal desire was to stay in town, this could be accomplished. In fact, he was willing to sign a deal that would carry him through retirement. Now there was just the little matter of agreeing on the exact amount warranted for the most sought-after anchor in the country. It was bound to be the largest contract ever paid a local anchor, in terms of the total package of salary, bonuses, and deferred payments. All that was left were the details. But at least from both parties' perspectives it was now possible.

Problem solved? Not quite. How could the station rationalize paying him at a scale so out of balance with their other personalities, whom they needed to nurture for the days after this anchor had retired? He might stay until retirement, but eventually that day would come and the station would have to have developed succession in order to maintain their leadership in the market. How could they explain this rich deal to the understudies and hopefuls? And how could they explain the deal to their network parent? After all, there were other markets that were even larger but weren't paying at this level. There were other major-market "stars" not getting a deal this lucrative. How could they not appear to have been held up by a superstar? (It's the same problem every baseball, football, basketball, and hockey team faces every time they award the "biggest contract ever" to the latest, greatest "most talented player ever.") The moment this deal was made, the station manager and his bosses could picture the headlines: "Local Anchor Signs Richest Deal in News Broadcasting," "TV Station Writes Biggest Paycheck Ever," and "MVP of Local News Inks Record Deal." Each headline would be more outrageous than the last, each one making the station management (and my client) more uncomfortable.

I knew it would come and the station brass knew it would come. Just the specter and fallout from it could undo the deal. So, though I represented the party who stood only to gain by the deal, my client and I put ourselves in the station's shoes and brainstormed as to what we would do if we were on that side. And we came up with an answer.

We had to find a way for the station to trumpet the deal instead of hiding from it or trying to minimize it. True, it would be the richest deal in the industry. But it would also be of record length. The station would "own" this superstar from now through his last day on the air, all the way through retirement. Why not let the station announce the deal as its coup instead of my client's? Let the station manager call a press conference to announce a different sort of headline: "Station Signs Most Sought-After Anchor to Contract for Life."

I even personally wrote a draft of the press release and gave it to the station's powers that be. They liked it. After tweaking it and rehearsing, they sent the release out to the press. And that's just how the story was reported. It was covered all over the country as a big deal, but the biggest news was the lifetime commitment, even more so than the dollars. Even the station could take bows for hanging on to this star. It was as if the Yankees signed Reggie Jackson, the Packers signed Brett Favre, or the Bulls signed Michael Jordan, not for a few years but for all of their playing days. Instead of the news being the unprecedented pay, the news became the unprecedented contract length. And instead of the glory and spotlight shining on the star, it shined on the management that made the deal. We recognized that it was important for the station to be able to "spin" the result to its benefit (and, frankly, the client was happy not to be in the spotlight over his new wealth). The station that had just agreed to pay a local news anchor more than any local anchor had ever made in the history of television didn't declare a holdup; it declared victory. As for the client, the anchor, defeat was never sweeter.

# CHAPTER SIXTEEN

# The Option to Play Ball

*How to Engage the Other Side in Exploring Options*

## FEAR NOT OPTIONS

SOME PEOPLE are afraid to create options because they fear that they will be forced to abide by those options. This attitude prevents the free flow of information. Remember that having or offering options is far different from actually exercising those options. (Just ask any dotcom employee who had plenty of stock options but was unable to exercise any of them because of the price.) Options are choices, possibilities, and ideas, not engraved-in-stone mandatories. They exist to facilitate movement in an otherwise stalled conversation or deal. At any time, either side is free to reject the options or further modify them. But by then, they may have already served their purpose, that is, getting the momentum unstuck. Generating options is never a waste of time.

> *"It is better to have options and not need them than to need them and not have them."*
>
> Mark Jankowski

## ENGAGING THE OTHER SIDE IN EXPLORING OPTIONS

One problem we sometimes face with difficult people is that de-spite our having spent prodigious time and energy generating op-tions, they may simply refuse to play the game. They stick to their "it's my way or the highway" approach. Their blanket refusal to think of or consider solutions can emanate from several sources:

- The Situationally Difficult person, while still in the heat of the moment, cannot see the benefit of considering options.
- The Strategically Difficult person has used the "there are no other options" ploy as a tactic in the past (perhaps successfully) and may be trying to use it again against you.
- The Simply Difficult person believes that he is in such a position of strength that he does not have to engage in an exploration of options.

Therefore, even if you have generated the greatest, most crea-tive, innovative, empathetic options in the world, they are under no obligation to consider them. After all, you came up with the options. And therein lies the problem. The other side has no stake in them. Unless you can engage the other person in the process of developing options, you may remain at an impasse. They have to comment on your ideas, critique them, or reject them. They have to put their ideas in. They have to get caught up in the process. They have to get into the sandbox with you and start building cas-tles. Or, to paraphrase L.B.J., "Don't ask me to be on the landing if I am not on the takeoff."

How, then, do you get the other (reluctant) side to engage in the process of creating options?

## METHODS FOR ENGAGING THE OTHER SIDE
## IN GENERATING OPTIONS

Get your adversaries to see the situation through your eyes. Many sage people have suggested, in many colorful ways, that we'd all be wiser if we could see the world through other people's eyes, walk a mile in their shoes, get inside their head, flip the mirror, find a way to truly experience other people's outlooks and feelings. If we're well intentioned, we may accomplish this kind of empathy from time to time. And we are wiser for it.

However, what is much more challenging is to get other people to see the world through our eyes. How do we get them to take a stroll in our moccasins, try on our hat, live under our roof, smoke our pipe, until they truly understand and feel what we experience? To say the least, this is always a difficult task. But not an impossible one. One of the least threatening ways to begin the process of "reversing roles" is to pose questions (rather than impose answers). Ask your opponents the following questions:

- *What would you do if you were on my side of the table?* Just come out and ask for a role swap. It's hypothetical but right to the point. Push them to try to see the situation from your perspective. This may not be comfortable for either side at first, because they might just tell you that having thought about it from your side, they still conclude you should give them everything that they want. You will need to be persistent. Ask follow-up questions such as "Do you see why, putting yourself in my place, that might not work for me?" or "If we did what you suggest, again, putting yourself in my place, what do you think would be my next reaction?"

• *What if*_____ *were not a problem?* Again, don't beat
around the bush. Just identify a sticking point and
theoretically remove it. (Remember, you don't have to
agree to this later. Theoretical is theoretical, not fact or fait
accompli.) This approach (temporarily) eliminates a
previous obstacle and allows the other side to get past a
roadblock that might otherwise have prevented continued
discussion of ideas. The minefield is gone. You are now
conversing in much safer territory. You may make progress
on the other critical issues that you could not even
approach while the sticking point was stuck. Then, once
more effective ideas have been generated or solutions have
been suggested, you will be operating from a stance of
mutual success. And then you may come back to the
original sticking point and find it isn't so impossible to
address. After all, now it's the only remaining open issue
in an almost done deal.

• *What would be wrong with doing it this way?* Instead of
avoiding criticism, invite it. Actually request it head-on.
Not only is it an uncommon approach, but it is disarming
to the other side. Most people cannot resist the chance to
tell us what's wrong with our views or proposals. When
cordially invited to tear our approach to pieces, they will
have a field day. But that's okay. In the process of their
criticizing to their heart's content and pointing out the
problems with your approach, they will often reveal
acceptable or preferred solutions. When they tell you what
they do not want, in a way they're telling you what options
they might consider perfectly acceptable. Let them tear
your approach apart . . . while creating options of their own
in the process.

The next real-life adventure—Ron's account of how a client faced unfortunate circumstances from which it appeared there was no positive outcome—illustrates the key points we teach about the value and use of options. In the end, the story shows how the situation could be turned around and saved by doggedly creating options and ultimately finding that elusive way out.

## THE OPTION TO PLAY BALL

In 1994 Michael Maas, my partner in the sports agency business, and I represented a client named Brian Anderson, a former first-round draft pick and left-handed pitcher with the then Anaheim Angels. When it came time for the club to renew Brian's contract, Michael was sent a new contract, or tender, for that year. Looking back, Michael says, "As soon as we received the tender, I knew the club had not tendered him properly. Under the rules of the Major League Baseball Collective Bargaining Agreement, we would have a good chance of having him declared a free agent. If you didn't tender a player properly, that was the consequence."

At that time the way a tender worked was this: Each year the baseball club had to "tender" or present the player with his contract for the next year by December 20. If the team didn't send the new contract by December 20, that player became a free agent. In addition, there were minimum standards or requirements that had to be met in the tender or it would be deemed an ineffective tender. The latter area was where the Angels erred that year. They made an offer on time but below the allowable minimum. A minimum allowable tender is determined by a somewhat complex formula. First, there is the current base salary. Then there are incentives that may be built into the contract. Depending on an individual's performance, a club is permitted to cut a player a maximum of 20 percent, either of total earnings for the prior year or on base salary, leaving the incentives in place. It is fairly rare that a team cuts a player's compensation, especially in a nonarbitration situation (meaning the team is under no threat of losing control of the player's salary).

Despite its rarity, however, the Angels did reduce Brian's pay, or attempted to do so. A pay reduction is a red flag. As Michael put it, "When I saw a pay cut, an alarm went off in my head and I started checking to see if everything had been done right." A pay cut is almost a contradictory message. Does the team want the player or not? If the team wants the player, it can keep him by paying no more than the previous season. Or if the team does not want the player, it can release him. But if it cuts the player's pay, it's saying, "We want to keep him, but *only if* we can get a discount."

After checking Brian's previous contract, comparing it with the new offer, running the numbers, and rerunning them, we began to believe the alarm that went off was not a false one. The tender package was below the minimum threshold for a renewal contract. It's not that the Angels weren't permitted to reduce Brian's pay, but they didn't do it by the major leagues' approved formula (as set forth in the collective bargaining agreement between the owners and the players). The team offered less than the lowest amount allowable. Now the question arose, "What do we do about it?"

We discussed the possible ramifications with Brian. Technically, this could render him a free agent and enable us to shop him throughout baseball for the best offer. (Free agency wasn't a sure thing, but chances were about 80 percent that the ruling would go that way.) Free agency or not, Brian's first choice was to remain in California. With that in mind, we arrived at a strategy. The first step was simply to inform the Angels that the offer had been tendered improperly. We didn't say, point blank, we were giving the team the chance to correct its error. We didn't say, if you don't correct it, Brian may become a free agent. We just said that an error had been made and waited for the response.

The Angels did respond, but not before the December 20 deadline. That was largely because their first offer had come in right at the deadline, so their revised offer was virtually bound to be late. As a result, now two errors had been committed: content of the first tender and timing of the revision. (*Note:* It was not uncommon for teams to make their offer so close to the drop-dead date that they almost never allowed time to correct or revise. It would seem to make sense to send the offers out by December 10 instead of by the twentieth, but year after year the clubs' offers came in at the eleventh hour. Today, as a result of this incident, major league baseball has what is commonly referred to as the Brian Anderson Rule: If a timely tender comes in that is improper in content, the club must be notified by the player and the club can correct the tender.)

We now found ourselves in the classic stuck circumstance we described earlier. They took a position, we took a position. They wouldn't budge, nor would we . . . Now what?

After the revised but late tender came in, we sat with Brian again and talked through the possibilities. He liked it in California, had been drafted by the Angels, played his entire career to that point with them, and, if paid fairly, would really prefer to stay with the team. We continued to maintain our position and strategy. We would aim to have him treated (and paid) as other clubs were treating players with similar on-field stats and who, like Brian, were not eligible for arbitration. The salary numbers, at the time, were in the $160,000 to $200,000 range for players not in a free-market or arbitration circumstance. That distinction is critical, since a free-market (or free-agent) situation might have brought as much as $1 million for Brian. We were not, on Brian's behalf, trying to test the upper limits; we just wanted him to be treated fairly and comparably with players of his caliber in his situation (that is, not as free agents and not as arbitration-eligible players).

Unfortunately, the Angels and the team's general manager, Bill Bavasi, didn't see it the same way we did. He was initially irritated and adamantly stuck to the revised tender offer, which was in the $120,000 range. We were looking for substantially more than that, up around $180,000. The Angels wouldn't budge. (Sound familiar? It's remarkable how similar most impasses are to each other.) Maybe they thought a player and his agent simply wouldn't proceed down the free-agency grievance route. Maybe they thought they would win in a free-agency grievance ruling. Maybe they determined that they were willing to lose Brian. Whatever they thought, they weren't changing their offer.

At this point, we were prepared to go the grievance route. We had the makings of a strong free-agency case. We had negotiated in good faith. The team had made an improper offer. After discussing the situation with Brian, we determined that our aim wasn't to force the showdown (yet). Instead, our aim was to turn a roadblock into a detour, take a longer route but one that would get us to our destination. We would create options. At our client's direction, we offered our first creative option: informing the team of the problem rather than blowing the whistle, thereby signaling cooperativeness, not weakness. We said, in effect, that we aren't rushing to arbitration and pursuit of free agency and its likely higher compensation, but rather giving you the opportunity to correct an error.

The team did respond, but too late. Again, we resisted crying foul. Again, we searched for a way to open the other side to our ideas. That led us to create our second option: checking comparables in the market and asking for like compensation. This would have allowed the team to save face, even have a win, at a nominal additional cost. However, that option was also rejected.

Should we continue to create options or now call for a showdown? Should we aim for free agency or should we brainstorm one more time? We thought it over long and hard. So far, we had been unable to engage the other side in exploring options. We analyzed the events and progress to this point to try to determine why.

Was the team's management reacting according to type by being Situationally, Strategically, or Simply Difficult? If the other side was reacting as Situationally Difficult, maybe it was too much in the heat of the moment to be open to options . . . yet. If it was reacting as Strategically Difficult, maybe it thought that refusing to be open to options was the most effective strategy for winning. If it was reacting as Simply Difficult, maybe it thought its position was so powerful, it simply need not even consider options.

Maybe these "maybes" were getting in the way. But certain realities were becoming clear: First, no longer was either side in the *Situational* heat of the moment. Second, a *Strategy* of refusing to be open to options was not proving productive. Finally, our adversaries *Simply* did not have an all-powerful position. So we decided it was worth it to try to come up with one more option . . . but we didn't yet know what it would be.

While we brainstormed, we maintained communication with the Angels' management. I continued to talk to Bill Bavasi, and Michael kept talking with the assistant general manager, Tim Meade. In our effort to get them to see the situation through our eyes, we asked them the direct and indirect questions we teach for engaging the other side:

What would you do if you were on our side of the table?

What if _____ were not a problem?

What would be wrong with doing it this way?

It was the last approach that opened the door. We put forth one more option, one more "what if," and that one elicited a glimmer of hope. We invited them to critique our new (and probably last) option.

Instead of filing for a free-agency hearing, we said we would talk to other ball clubs to see if they would offer Brian Anderson a good contract package and compensate the Angels with good players. We would essentially preshop the market a little, since we, the Angels, and other clubs knew full well that Brian's becoming a free agent would bring him a heftier price tag and would offer no compensation to the Angels.

There were a few teams that Brian found attractive. We submitted a list to the Angels, offering, in effect, a chance for them to criticize, take apart, and rebuild our idea. The Angels researched the list and proceeded with Cleveland, Brian's hometown. They then opened talks with the Indians' general manager, in some part because they were beginning to believe they might really lose Brian (though they didn't admit it), but they also knew that if the Indians offered a good contract, Brian would go there, and they hoped the Indians would present an acceptable player-talent exchange. In fact, the Angels did find a good player swap and then gave us permission to talk contract terms with Cleveland. This last option did what none of the others had done. It gave the other side the feeling of control.

And that is how the situation was resolved, through creative options rather than ultimatums. The Angels had made an improper offer, then made an attempt, though late, to correct it and, as a result of the tardiness of the amended offer, actually compounded the error, leaving our client open to arbitration and a likely declaration of free agency. Rather than forcing a showdown, we carefully planned and executed a strategy that offered a series of thoughtful, imaginative options. Even in the face of seemingly stubborn rebuffs of our first option, and then our second, we still pursued our strategy further, until it finally became clear to the other side that our options might be the most appealing, least harmful outcome for them, as well as for our client.

Had we gone the showdown route, what might have happened? We'd have entered the grievance procedure. Rather than endure the process, the Angels might have capitulated with a market-competitive contract offer but not been happy about it. Or they might have waited for a ruling, likely one that would render Brian a free agent, thereby losing him to another team without compensation. Brian would have been paid well, but not necessarily in a location of his preference. Or if, against the odds, the Angels had prevailed in the grievance, they would have retained a player in a less than ideal frame of mind, essentially playing for a team and for compensation against his will.

All of the above were, in some ways, negative results. However, at one point it seemed as if there was no other way out or at least no *good* way out. Bill Bavasi and Tim Meade are smart, honest baseball guys who clearly thought they were in the right. They weren't just going to wake up one day, in the heat of the negotiations, and see things our way. However, if you asked them today about the outcome, they'd probably say we all found a good solution to a bad situation. When two sides are involved in an emotionally charged, high-stakes, competitive encounter, you can't ask for more than a way out. That's what creative options are all about—finding an exit in a room that seems to have no doors. Try the window. Look for a skylight. Knock down a wall (or, as in the rainstorm story, give your car to your friend to drive the elderly woman to the hospital while you get to know the love of your life). Sometimes the right answers aren't obvious. They require an open mind and a good imagination. That's why they're called creative options.

*Postscript:* You often don't really know if the other side found the solution to be as reasonable as you did until a lot of time has passed. Later in 2002, I needed tickets for my family to see *The Lion King* in New York. Through Cal Ripken's office, we contacted Tim Meade, who was still with the Angels, and he contacted Disney, which owned both the Angels and *The Lion King*. Believe me, if we'd left a negative feeling after our negotiation for Brian Anderson, my family wouldn't have been sitting in the theater at all . . . in the balcony, behind a pole, or even in the concession stand. But it was a win for both sides. And we sat in the center of the orchestra section, giving a standing ovation for *The Lion King* . . . and for finding creative options.

*Post Postscript:* Just in case we thought the good feelings between the parties were only off the baseball field, we found ourselves in face-to-face player contract negotiations with the same Bill Bavasi just before the 2004 season. If he had held a grudge, surely it would show in this circumstance. Bill had moved on from the Angels to the Seattle Mariners, serving as their general manager and executive vice president of baseball operations. We were representing Mariners catcher Ben Davis for his new contract with the team, and outfielder Raul Ibanez, coming to the Mariners from the Kansas City Royals. In both cases, we had to deal directly with Bill . . . and he with us. In both cases, we naturally wanted the best deal for our players and he wanted the best deal for his club, which by definition were almost opposite financially. But despite the expected push and pull of negotiation, our previous relationship wasn't a minus but rather was a plus. We all knew and trusted one another *because* of our past experience. The creative options of the Brian Anderson incident paid dividends for other ballplayers and management well after the initial negotiation was completed.

# CHAPTER SEVENTEEN

# I Said/He Said

*Ending Without Escalating*

## NOW WHAT? . . .

Okay, you have learned, practiced, and dutifully tried it all—
every technique, tactic, maneuver, and lesson of N.I.C.E.—
with the utmost sincerity, open-mindedness, and flexibility. And
you now sit across the table from . . . the same stubborn, unreasonable, irrational, immovable B.T.I.P. you started with. He or she is
as entrenched than ever. To every overture you have made, he or
she has listened (or not), weighed your approach (or not), considered compromise (or not), and ultimately offered the equivalent of
a two-word response (and the words are not "happy birthday").
Despite your best efforts, you have gone from stuck to still stuck.

Now what do you say to that B.T.I.P.? Can you finally yell and
scream? Can you throw a heavy object? Is it okay to tell everyone
he or she associates with what an unreasonable maniac he or she
is? Can you send out a mass e-mail? Tip off *60 Minutes*? Sabotage
his business? Kidnap his cat? Tell her mom?

You will be tempted. It's only human. But we advise against all
of the above.

While we would like to say we promise a 100 percent success
rate, there are difficult people who remain steadfastly difficult.

And, unfortunately, the rest of us who must deal with them remain stuck. After you've exhausted every method available, naturally you get frustrated. Very, very, very frustrated. You want your own pound of flesh. You want to make them pay. You fantasize complex plots that end in their demise. You play out diabolical scenes in which they're humiliated. You picture them coming back to you, begging, pleading, crawling on their knees.

*Our advice:* Engage in fantasy to vent your feelings; just don't act out your fantasies. After you've entertained yourself with your private movie plots, return to reality and think ahead.

## REVENGE CAN BACKFIRE

The desire for revenge may be natural, but inherent in it is the possibility that though your intention is to get even with the other person, it can cause *you* further damage. It can prolong your agony by keeping you engaged in a very negative, poisoned encounter. The best thing you can do for yourself—and for any future encounters with this individual—is to end without escalating. Simply walking away can put the incident exactly where it belongs, behind you. Sure, that sounds very rational, but it is hard to carry out for logical reasons:

- We often want to teach the difficult person a "lesson." ("Surely, she will see the error of her ways once I publicly embarrass her.")
- We sometimes feel we have no other alternatives than to fight. ("Fine, if he says 'No new deal,' then I'll screw up our current deal.")
- We do not realize that an ending is not always an ending. ("What? I could end up dealing with this person again?")

You may recall an earlier story in which Mark and I were dealing with the Fortune 500 multinational outsourcing services company and a human resources executive who we felt wasn't treating us honorably and fairly. Mark was unable to neutralize his emotions (and I was unable to influence him to do so). He blew up when this particularly difficult person lied and cost us the opportunity to win a deal. We were determined to "teach that woman a lesson" by setting out to get her fired. We systematically identified every contact point we had within the company and communicated to management what we considered to be behavior by this individual that was inconsistent with the values of the company and with business ethics in general. That's the sophisticated version. In plain English, we bad-mouthed the person who had lied. Unfortunately, despite the fact that the chairman did not agree with the type of behavior exhibited by his employee, despite his sympathy to our position, in the end, he backed his employee and the employee's decision. In the end, all of the bad-mouthing ricocheted back to damage those trying to get revenge. Instead of getting the perpetrator fired, instead of maintaining our seminar contract with the company, it did just the opposite. Yes, we felt (temporarily) great after our tirade (fantasizing the comeuppance for the bad guy), but ultimately our behavior only served to cause a rift between our company and our (now former) client that could not be mended. Even *after* this difficult person left our old client, the negative feelings surrounding the attempted revenge remained. The company politely, but consistently, ignored our overtures for continued seminars.

In trying to teach a lesson, we learned one ourselves. We would have been much better served *not* to escalate the situation. Had Mark stepped back and successfully neutralized emotions, had I stepped in and helped him neutralize, had we both simply let the issue lie for a while, the outcome might well have been different. No matter what we did, we were going to lose that particular contract. But we were not necessarily predestined to be rejected for any and all future contracts. And, in fact, when our nemesis left the company, had we had unsullied relations with the company, we would have been in a position to return and offer our services to those same key management contacts (who had liked our services) and we likely would have succeeded in winning renewed business. Once again, lesson learned . . . by the teacher.

Mark and I came by this temptation to escalate and get even naturally. It happens to all of us. And it takes a lot of discipline and determination to resist our human nature. Somewhere in our genetic makeup must exist the "revenge gene." As the following story demonstrates, the wind was not blowing very hard when this son's apple fell from the proverbial parental tree.

## THE LANDLORD VERSUS THE TATTOO ARTIST

When I was a young man, my father, Joe, had taken on a part-time vocation as a landlord. Joe Jankowski considered himself a fair, no-nonsense kind of businessman. He would do business with anyone as long as the other party lived up to the terms of the lease. So he had no qualms about renting a little shop to a big, tough, ugly, multiply tattooed guy who made his living putting hideous, unsavory, threatening tattoos on people's various body parts. It wasn't the tattoos that got to my father. It was the tattooer's failure to pay the rent. It wasn't even the first month the tattooer got behind. It was the second, third, fourth, and eventually twelfth month behind. Finally, Joe did what he did with all delinquent tenants. He started the eviction process. It took months, but finally he was able to evict the big, tough, ugly tattooer. And then Joe pursued him for the lost rent—a little less than $1,000—and won a legal judgment against him.

Victory, right? Joe showed the bully and got his money, right? End of story, right?

Wrong, wrong, wrong. Even though Joe had the legal judgment, he still had to collect his money. Month after month, Joe sent threatening letters. Month after month, the tattooer ignored his debt. I told my father he was never going to get the money, no matter how hard he tried. He would've been better off walking away, but my father refused to do so. The big, tough, ugly tattooer got mad and frightening (like his tattoos). First, the thinly veiled threats began. "I wouldn't try to have me evicted. I wouldn't want any harm to come to you." Soon the tattooer took the veil off of his threats. "Come near me and I'll break your legs." Would he ever pay? Joe's reaction to a bully who didn't pay his rent had been to fight. Unfortunately, that reaction put him in harm's way.

Finally, the tattooer left town . . . without paying the back rent and not before trashing the place. Was the fight worth it? Or might there have been a better solution?

## THE WALKAWAY ALTERNATIVE

When exploring the option of walking away, many people will tell us, "I wish I could, but I have no alternative but to fight back," and they offer the following reasons:

"If I don't fight back, I could lose my job."
"I do not know how I would support myself if I left my spouse/partner/associate/boss."

"This person is family and I cannot just walk away from
family."

These reasons are all legitimate, sincere, and serious impediments to
walking away from a difficult person or situation. We understand
that it may not be viable or realistic to walk away *immediately* (the
moment you realize your efforts are fruitless) from a difficult person. However, pragmatists that we are, we advocate taking a
longer-term view, and to those who say they simply cannot walk
away, we respond as follows:

- If you cannot walk away because you need your job, you
  may need to continue to deal with the difficult person until
  you find another job.
- If you do not see a way to support yourself in the event
  you leave a spouse or partner, start exploring how to
  prepare yourself to do so.
- Even if the difficult person is part of your family, you
  should begin to find means to isolate or limit your exposure
  to that person.

Walking away is *always* an option, even if it is not an option
that can be executed immediately. Remember the story we told
called "The Boss from Hell" about one of our seminar participants
who worked for a tyrannical, demanding, ranting, raving, unrelenting, nasty ogre (and those were his good qualities). As we counseled and taught, she had dutifully applied each and every lesson of
N.I.C.E. and had hit a wall. He remained as tyrannical, demanding, ranting, raving, and unrelenting as ever. She felt trapped because she could not afford to lose her job and she could not support
herself on her own. (It could only have been worse if the despotic

boss had been her brother—family she felt she couldn't abandon.)
As you may recall, we coached her through the process of taking
inventory on her life, values, and skills so she could explore other
career options. There were several professional alternatives. She
realized she could live on less money if she had to. She could
change career paths if need be. But there were even some attractive
job opportunities available, some of which would pay her as well,
if not better. Because she had prepared herself for a walkaway, by
the time she met with her boss, she was not really trapped. In fact,
she was free. Her story, and its resolution, made for a perfect case
study in (1) the necessity and inherent power in having the option
to walk away and (2) the specific ways to prepare oneself to walk,
eventually, even if not immediately.

### How to Prepare for the Walkaway

1. Enlist a friend/coach to act as an objective third party. (If
you think you're trapped, it will be hard for you to
think/act objectively on your own.)
2. Take inventory on what power the other person seems to
have over you.
3. Step back (with help from your friend/coach) and
coolly assess what power the other person *really* has
over you.
4. Take inventory on what power you possess.
5. Lay out a worst-case scenario. What will happen if
you walk. (This is one you can do better than the third-
party friend/coach. No one can lay out a worse worst case
than you.)
6. List the critical issues to be dealt with prior to a
walkaway, such as incurring expenses and saving money,

replacing a lost customer/deal, exploring jobs and
determining career impact, and taking account of personal
fallout.

7. List actions to be taken to address each critical issue.

8. Set a (realistic) timetable. Monitor with friend/coach and
adjust to changing circumstances.

Preparing for the walkaway is also a method for keeping your
sanity while you remain in the untenable situation. Just knowing
you are planning for the time when you will be free of this unpleasant person or force in your life can keep your mind and attitude
intact.

## THE END? MAYBE OR MAYBE NOT

Perhaps the single most compelling reason for ending without escalating is that the end often isn't as final as it sounds. It's the end
for now—the pause, hiatus, conclusion to date, last word until the
next word, Part I of a miniseries. The deal that is pronounced dead
today often comes back to life next year when new ownership
takes over. The takeover bid that is rebuffed by the board may be
embraced a few months later when either the target company is
weaker or the acquirer's offer goes up. The personal relationship
that soured may somehow sweeten when the other party discovers
that maybe he or she needs you again. Baseball manager Billy
Martin was hired and fired, rehired and refired, and then hired
yet again by George Steinbrenner and the New York Yankees (and,
finally, fired one last time). The nation rejected Richard Nixon
for president in 1960 and his political career was over . . . until
1968, when he was elected by a substantial majority. Simon and

Garfunkel split up and then reunited. Every year many divorced men and women remarry the same person they once divorced.

> *It ain't over till it's over.*
>
> Yogi Berra

## JUST IN CASE . . .

Ending without escalating allows you to put the bad experience behind you (for now) but leaves the door open to that unpredictable future encounter. You haven't burned bridges, and you just didn't jump off one either.

The risk in escalating—fighting back, getting even, teaching a lesson, or trying to punish the other person—is that you never know when, where, or how you will run into that person again. When and if you do, put yourself in a position to make your deal then, the deal you thought was dead. And as we learned from Walt Disney, "It's a small world after all."

Here is a classic story of ending without escalating. Oh, we were tempted to "go to the mattresses," but we resisted that temptation. Ron relives the experience to show the value—in certain instances—of walking away without pouring gasoline on the fire.

## I SAID/HE SAID
### *A Battle of Memories Not Worth Waging*

In the first edition of our previous book, *The Power of Nice,* we told a story that illustrated the negative results of giving in to the temptation to get even, to go for a win-lose outcome. I had been Oprah Winfrey's agent when her career began to blossom on a local level and helped navigate her initial entry into the Chicago market. Shortly thereafter, I lost her as a client to another agent, then gave in to peer pressure from my partners and pursued—and won—lost revenue, but I also lost a long-term valuable personal relationship in the process. (Too often win-lose situations end up more as a loss than a win.) While the personal rapport was later repaired, the lesson of the story is that the short-term win was overshadowed by the longer-term loss.

But the story taught another lesson. In writing it, we had referred to Oprah's hiring of the new agent in Chicago (who later became a television executive). Evidently, my version of the process of changing her agent representation, as pieced together from various parties' recollections, differed significantly from the version maintained by the agent himself. When he read this section of the book, he took great exception to it and contacted me to register his serious disagreement. I was surprised by his reaction but listened to his concerns and told him I would get back to him.

Frankly, my first reaction was to dispute his version. I had told the story as I recalled it. I felt confident that my recollection was accurate. To assess the best course of action, I gathered my human resources, including Mark and my good friend and skilled litigator, Paul Sandler. Mark probed me on the substance of the story again.

He asked if I was comfortable with my version. I said yes but noted that no one's memory is perfect. I then asked Paul what the possible consequences might be. He conjectured as follows: The agent could ask us to delete the story from the book or revise it to satisfy his objections. If we refused, he might pursue the matter, threatening to sue. If we again refused to acquiesce, he could go forward and file suit for an inaccurate depiction of the events and possible resulting damages. Paul suggested the matter could become protracted, expensive, and very unpleasant. Would we prevail in court? Perhaps. It would depend upon whose version of the story could be better corroborated, ours or the agent's. We decided to think about it overnight.

In the meantime, I contacted our publisher and spoke to our editor. He consulted his people and determined that any action would be our decision. He did, however, offer that if it became a high-profile legal battle, ironically, the resulting publicity might help sell books.

Mark, Paul, and I regrouped a day or so later. We looked at our options. We could gird ourselves for possible battle, doing our best to reconstruct our version of the story. I had already asked some colleagues who had been involved to check their recollections of the story. They were consistent with mine but, as age dims memories, hardly perfect. And, if battle ensued, we could maintain that our story did no damage to the agent turned television executive. As for taking the story out of the book, it was too late, as the book had already gone to press and had been shipped to stores. In fact, initial sales to retailers and early reviews were very strong. The publisher was already about to do a second printing and shortly add a paperback edition. And, of course, there was no need to take the story out if we were sure of its accuracy. We could just hold our ground, battle or no battle, protracted or brief, expensive or cheap, unpleasant or not, until it reached an end. We could let the end escalate . . . and escalate . . . and escalate.

But maybe it wasn't worth it. Maybe my version wasn't exactly, precisely 100 percent flawlessly accurate. Maybe the agent's version was just as accurate. Maybe my colleagues' memories weren't perfect. Maybe the substance of the story was correct, but one fact was off. We are, after all, only human. What good would the escalation do? What would be gained? On the other hand, what if we decided just to put this issue behind us? Could I apologize to this man for any inaccuracy or injustice, advertent or not, done him? Now that we knew we had another edition coming out, could we revise the story to his satisfaction and put it in the next edition? Could we end but *without* escalating?

That is exactly what we opted to do. I spelled out the details in a letter to him that concluded with the following line: "I hope that somehow our paths cross and that we can find ways to build bridges together and put this whole experience behind us."

And the television executive graciously agreed to that solution. In fact, we must have built a future bridge, because before putting this further lesson into this book, we sought and got his blessing on the updated story you just read.

## The End . . . without escalating

# ACKNOWLEDGMENTS

Jim Dale has been a partner in our writing efforts and has become a friend and advisor as well. Without him this book would still be a work in progress.

We also are indebted to our agent, David Black, for his guidance and his advocacy of our cause, and to Michael Winger, for his thoughtful research assistance. Our editor, John Mahaney, has been a wise and patient guide through the process. Paul Sandler, Michael Maas, Judge Lawrence Rodowsky, Steve Bisciotti, Bill Polian, Randy Levine, Michael Bryant, and Jim Novick also provided us valuable insight and support.

Thanks also go to our great team at the Shapiro Negotiations Institute who sometimes must practice the art of dealing with impossible people when dealing with us.

Our wives, Cathi and Lori, have always been there for us as we worked through this process, and we thank them for that and so much more.

And finally, many others, too numerous to name, assisted us during the long process and helped make this book possible. We thank them.

# INDEX

RONALD M. SHAPIRO, Esq., is coauthor of the award-winning book *The Power of Nice: How to Negotiate So Everyone Wins—Especially You* and the cofounder of the Shapiro Negotiations Institute, which has trained more than 250,000 individuals worldwide in the art of negotiation, dealing with difficult personalities, and enhancing listening skills. He is known as "one of baseball's most respected agent-attorneys" *(USA Today)* and is one of the nation's premier motivational speakers and negotiations experts. He has used his extensive experience in negotiations and dealing with difficult personalities to settle a major symphony orchestra strike, defuse racial tension in a metropolitan police department, and help end Major League Baseball's last historic labor deadlock. Both the author of and the subject of numerous articles, Shapiro is committed to public and civic matters and has chaired more than twenty-five boards of charitable and community organizations.

MARK A. JANKOWSKI, Esq., is coauthor of *The Power of Nice* and cofounder of the Shapiro Negotiations Institute. He has been engaged to deliver negotiations and conflict resolution seminars on six continents and has worked with some of America's leading businesses, including GenRe (a Berkshire-Hathaway Company), MBNA America, Gillette, and Black and Decker. A graduate of Harvard University and the University of Virginia School of Law, he has also taught negotiation programs at Johns Hopkins University and the Wharton School of Business. Jankowski has contributed to articles in *Fortune, Reader's Digest,* and *Smart Money* magazine.

Printed in the United States
by Baker & Taylor Publisher Services